Riders Up!
Rene Riera, Jr.

Published by:

Rene Riera, Jr.
Miami, FL

ISBN: **10: 0692728899**

First Edition © 2016 by Rene Riera, Jr.

All right reserved. No part of this publication may be reproduced, stored in a retrieval system, or transmitted in any form or by any means, electronic, mechanical, photocopying, recording, scanning, or otherwise, except as permitted under Sections 107 or 108 of the 1976 United States Copyright Act, without the prior written permission of the publisher. Requests to the publisher for permission should be addressed to rriera2@bellsouth.net.

PART ONE
2
3
4
5
6
7
PART TWO
9
10
PART THREE
12
PART FOUR
14
15
PART FIVE
PART SIX
18
19
20
21
22
23
24
PART SEVEN
26
27
28
PART EIGHT
30
PART NINE
32
33
34
35
36
37
38
EPILOGUE

To Olga and Sylvia,
two halves that make me whole

PART ONE

"Be nice. Don't be like my wife," jested the handler as he tried to calm the anxious thoroughbred in the stall of the starting gate. The jockey was crouched and ready, as the starter squeezed a pair of prongs that broke the electric circuit keeping the front doors closed. Seconds later, as the last horse was loaded, the starter released the prongs, and the front doors opened simultaneous with the ringing of a loud bell. In an instant, the field of eight horses broke running. Friday's seventh race at Boston's Suffolk Downs was off.

The early June thunderstorm had left the racing surface a quagmire. Racing at an average of 35 miles per hour perched on a horse's back on a saddle often weighing less than two pounds is an ever-present risk for riders and their mounts, more so under sloppy and slippery conditions. It's a daunting task and along with the mindset that the show must go on, jockeys understand the danger of their craft accepting it in trade for the thrills, the fame, and the money.

Breaking from the #5 post position, *Onlythelonely,* with apprentice Luke Nodarse aboard, was a length in front of the field within the first several strides of the six-furlong event.

Trying to conserve the horse's speed, Luke took a long hold of the reins and deftly eased his mount back, allowing #1 and #3 to engage him from the inside. As the three horses reached the green and white 5/8 pole, they were nose to nose, but while the other two jockeys were urging their mounts to maintain their positions, Nodarse sat motionless still saving his horse.

Passing the red and white half-mile pole, Nodarse reduced the hold on his mount and began to inch away from the two rivals on his inside. At the same time, the #6 horse, with the veteran Sam Bruno aboard, loomed boldly on the outside to overtake Nodarse and the other two and quickly started to drop in without sufficient clearance.

Aware of the upcoming turn, when the horses' natural instinct is to change leads from right to left to properly navigate the bend, Nodarse yelled to Bruno, "I've got two inside." Oblivious to his rivals' tight spot, Bruno continued urging his mount inward, jamming the three horses on his inside against one another with the immovable inside rail acting as a barrier.

"No-no-no-no-n—!" The words of warning never fully made it out of his mouth. In an instant, the left front hoof of Nodarse's mount clipped a hind heel of Bruno's horse, causing the animal to stumble and fall catapulting Nodarse heavily into the sloppy racetrack. In quick succession, the two horses closer to the rail, unable to avoid the fallen horse and rider, also went down.

The last jockey to fall was shaken up but escaped unscathed, and quickly sat up. The other two riders lay prone on the sloppy ground; one of them groaning in pain, the other lost consciousness after a horse's hoof hit his fiberglass helmet leaving a bleeding gash on the left side of his head. Two of the riderless horses got up and ran loose; the third one suffered irreparable damage in a front leg, remained down and soon was humanely euthanized by the track veterinarian.

In the wake of the catastrophe, riding the second favorite in the race, Sam Bruno went on to finish fourth after causing the spill, only to have his mount disqualified and the jockey later suspended by the stewards. But the job got done. The 3-5 favorite with Nodarse up was eliminated, and the three horses with the longest odds finished 1-2-3. A total of 57 mutuel tickets in a variety of denominations were sold on the winning trifecta combination, but none over twenty dollars for fear of attracting attention. The neat score netted over $168,000 to the manipulators of the race. For his part in the coup, Bruno was paid $700 and a two-dollar trifecta ticket worth $1340.20.

Within moments, the ambulance following the field of horses from the start of the race came to the aid of the downed riders. Paramedics quickly assessed each jockey's condition, concluding instantly that Nodarse was the most critical. One of the paramedics radioed for backup. The unhurt jockey brushed himself off and was helped up to climb aboard the veterinarian's pickup truck, which also followed the field from the beginning of the race while paramedics quickly fixed Nodarse with a cervical collar and artificial respiration; a bandage was applied to the wound on his head. Careful to avoid unnecessary movement, he was transferred to a long spine board. With help from the starting gate crew, the jockey was secured in the ambulance as the other less injured rider awaited the arrival of the backup emergency vehicle moments later.

Less than fifteen minutes after the horrific spill, the wailing siren of the first ambulance arrived at the emergency entrance of Massachusetts General Hospital. Still semi-conscious, Nodarse was assessed by the waiting trauma team, rapidly transferred to a stretcher and rushed to an operating room as a desperate elderly priest tried to keep in step with the gurney ready to administer the sacrament of the sick.

Nearly two hours passed. Nodarse's agent, Paul Dwyer, had been pacing the emergency room when finally, he was approached by medical staff to inform him the jockey was stabilized but was still being examined; no specific injuries were disclosed.
"Does he have any family?" asked the medic.

"His mother lives a couple of hours away. I called her; she's on her way," answered Dwyer. "By the way, how is the other rider?" the agent asked.

"He's badly bruised and sore, but nothing's broken. We're keeping him overnight to keep an eye on him. His wife is with him now," said the young doctor before rushing back around the corner of the hallway.

2

The following morning, Luke squinted into the light to see his mother's worried face watching over him. His lips moved to whisper "Hi, Mom." She broke into a light smile as she said, "My son," gently kissing his cheek. "I need to tell the nurse you're awake; I'll be right back."

The nurse entered the room followed by Mrs. Nodarse. She leaned over and said, "Hello, Luke; my name is Nancy," as she gently put a thermometer between his lips, and reached for the fabric cuff she would wrap around his arm to check his blood pressure.

"Try not to move, honey." She then fussed with the tubes attached to his left arm.

"What's wrong with me?" Luke asked gravelly.

"The doctor will be here to talk to you in a little while, dear." She wrote something on the clipboard at the foot of the bed, looking toward Mrs. Nodarse, and said, "Mom, I'll be outside if you need me."

When Luke tried to speak to his mother, his chest ached. The slightest movement caused pain. He sensed the cast on his right leg and a bandage on the left side of his head. He managed to say "Pretty banged up, huh Mom."

His mother said, "You'll be all right Luke. Just rest."

Later that morning, two doctors and nurse Nancy came into the room. They were followed by Luke's grandparents who had just arrived.

The older doctor made the introductions, "Hello, Luke. I'm Dr. Sloane. I'm here with Dr. Malcolm. You had us pretty worried last night." The older doctor's measured and soothing cadence projected his prominence as head of the Sports Medicine Department at MGH.

"What's wrong with me?" Luke struggled to ask, feeling the pain on his chest.

"Luke, you were very lucky. All of the tests performed on you disclosed no major injuries. At first, we feared internal bleeding." Dr. Sloane continued, "but there's severe bruising. You fractured three ribs, which we're sure will be very painful for a while, so it is very important you limit any unnecessary movement."

The doctor dismissed Luke's attempt to speak and continued, "You have other damage young man. You also fractured your right leg, which we treated with a plastic cast for now. Last, you have a laceration on the left side of your head just above your ear, which required 12 stitches. It is obvious your skull-cap protected you from more serious injury in that area."

The younger Dr. Malcolm chimed in, "All in all, you were very fortunate. We heard it was a very bad spill."

Dr. Sloane placed his index finger on Luke's right hand and asked him to squeeze. He then moved to the foot of the bed, took his pen from his breast pocket and ran it across the toes of the right foot. "Can you feel that?" Luke mouthed, "Yes." Then, moving to the other foot, he ran the pen from the bottom up, which caused Luke to curl his toes. "I guess you feel that too." The doctor continued to the other side of the bed and again placed his finger on the young man's left hand. "Squeeze," he said.

"You will be fine," he said as he stepped back. Dr. Malcolm will check with you later today, and we'll see you here for the next two or three days. Okay?" The doctor managed a slight smile.

"When can I ride again?" asked Luke, as Dr. Sloane turned away.

"Young man, let us concentrate on getting you cured. But to answer your question, you will be able to return to all your normal activities within six to eight weeks if all goes accordingly."

The two doctors exited the room stopping in the hallway where they briefly spoke to Mrs. Nodarse in a hushed tone. Her parents walked toward their injured grandson, the grandmother clutching rosary beads in her right hand.

3

Four years earlier, in his second year of high school, Luke Nodarse worked part time at a grocery store near his home. The store sold Cuban and Latin American products to the small community of immigrants from those countries. Luke bagged groceries and helped out in general, saving all his money to buy a car upon graduation.

One Sunday morning, while working the cash register, the lone shopper in the store unloaded his shopping cart on the counter. The man wore a white western hat and a big silver buckle on his belt.

As he watched young Luke bagging the groceries, speaking with a Cuban accent like Luke's older relatives, the middle-aged man asked, "Somebody told me about this store. It's my first time here," said the stranger. "Slow today? What time do you close?"

"On Sundays, usually around 4:00," Luke responded.

"Yeah, that's about the time I get back to my barn to feed my horses," said the man. "Say, do you like horses?"

"I do, but there are no horses around here," Luke answered.

"You know you're small enough to be a jockey. Anybody ever tell you that?"

Luke shook his head as the man continued, "I'm going to be in the city again next Sunday. If you can take the time off, I'll meet you here at the store about the same time and take you to see my horses at the track where I work. Would you like that? My name is Jacinto Hernandez," he said, stretching his hand out to shake Luke's.

"I'd like that," said the teenager smiling, "I'm Luke."

As scheduled, Luke met Jacinto the following week. In those days there was no horse racing on Sundays; it was a day of rest for stable employees and their horses, and a chance for horse bettors to take a break from the action. The dark-haired Luke got in the car, and 25 minutes later, Jacinto waved to the guard at the Lincoln Downs stable gate entrance, continuing to barn F.

As they got out of the car, Luke saw a group of men laughing and speaking Spanish walking toward a building with a sign that read "Track Kitchen." He followed Jacinto to the barn.

"What do you think of these horses?" a proud Jacinto said as he patted the neck of the gray horse in the first stall.

"Do you own all of them?" asked the teenager.

"No, no. I just work here. I'm a groom; I take care of these first four. Three other guys, who should be here at any minute, look after four horses each."

Luke watched as Jacinto went from stall to stall and with a pitch fork picked up each animal's refuse, discarding it into a plastic tub. Jacinto then emptied a bag of oats and put a strong smelling jug of liquid that looked like molasses and boxes of other ingredients into a wheelbarrow. He then cut the strings of a bale of hay to load the racks that would later be tied up in a corner of each horse's stall.

"Here, you can help me. Just push the wheelbarrow from stall to stall as I scoop grain in the feed tubs." As he said this, three other men entered the shedrow. They were younger than Jacinto.

"Hey, muchachos, come meet the next great jockey!" shouted Jacinto as the men came closer and shook Luke's hand. They all spoke with Spanish accents.

"Where're you from, man?" asked the one called Nacho. *Maybe the guy likes chips*, thought Luke.

"I'm from Providence. I met Jacinto at the store where I work," Luke answered.

Another one called Miguel said, "Nodarse is a Spanish name. Do you speak Spanish, my man?"

"Not really. I understand a little. We speak mostly English at home."

To which the man said, "How about that, a family of gringos." They all laughed as they went to take care of their horses.

On the way back to the city, Luke asked many questions, but in particular, "How come I didn't see any jockeys at the track?"

"Luke, jockeys are like royalty. Yeah, they come out in the mornings and sometimes exercise a couple of horses. Their real work is in the afternoons riding races and making lots of money."

When they arrived back to the store, Luke thanked Jacinto and said, "The next time you come shopping, I'll buy you a cold drink."
"Yeah, I do like a cold beer once in a while," Jacinto said with a wink. They both laughed and said goodbye.

4

His employment at the grocery store lasted almost a year. The owner told Luke the day before that business was not going the way he had expected. The little market catering to Cubans and other Latin Americans was to be closed at the end of the month. Many of his customers said they hated the cold winters and snowstorms while working in factories for little money and decided to try their luck farther south. Even if their financial situation didn't improve, at least the winters wouldn't be as severe.

The store had never done much business for sure, and after a couple of days when nickels and dimes of penny candy were the only sales, the owner decided to let the lease of the locale run out at the end of the month and go back to work at the cast iron plant north of the city.

Luke told his mother about losing the job when he got home. She said she would ask her boss if there was maybe something he could do in the stock room of the store where she worked downtown. But that was a longshot anyway. Luke didn't see himself working in the stockroom of a women's lingerie shop. With winter coming, maybe a paper route and shoveling snow would have to do.

On his last day of work, he came home to find a long-time friend of the family sitting at the dining room table having coffee with his grandparents, rehashing and laughing about stories from the old country the way they always did whenever they got together. Middle-aged Jose Gomez was a short-order cook at a restaurant downtown, not far from where Luke's mother worked.

When Jose started saying his goodbyes, which usually lasted about 20 minutes, Luke asked him if maybe they needed a waiter or even a dishwasher where he worked.

Jose replied, "I've been working at O'Rourke's for seven years; they love me there. I think I can help you out."

The next day, Jose called and asked Luke if he could come to the restaurant after school the following day. The manager of the restaurant wanted to meet him before offering him a job.

"Heck yes, Jose, I'll walk down there. I do it with my friends all the time when we go to the movies downtown."

After school the following Monday, Luke started his job at O'Rourke's Restaurant. He was their new part-time busboy and dishwasher. At 95 cents per hour and all you could eat free, life was good!

As the weeks passed, Luke enjoyed his job, especially when one of the nearby offices phoned in an order and Luke was called on to make the delivery. The tips were great.

As his sixteenth birthday neared, Jose promised he would teach him how to drive. More and more, Luke saw Jose as the father he had lost at the age of six when his parents divorced. At first, his dad would take Luke for the day now and then. But that ended years before; Luke hadn't seen his father in a long time.

Winter came, and Luke looked forward to summer vacation when he could start working full time at the restaurant, hoping to have his learner's permit by then.

As he went to pick up a tray of dirty dishes at the restaurant one afternoon, Luke saw the manager, working the cash register, walk to the kitchen from around the corner and call to Jose that he had a visitor. Walking out to the dining room, Luke saw a handsome young man not much taller than himself, wearing what looked like tailored clothes and trendy shoes; his shiny black hair stylishly combed. Jose came out from the kitchen, and when he saw the visitor, he called out, "Mickey!" and they cheerfully hugged each other like they were best friends.

Sitting on the counter catching up, Luke heard the visitor tell Jose he was in town for the start of Lincoln. On his next trip to retrieve a tray of dirty dishes, Jose called Luke over, "Luke, meet my brother Mickey. He just got in town." They shook hands and exchanged hellos. Luke excused himself and took the tray of dirty dishes back to the kitchen.

Back in the kitchen, the restaurant's chef, Charlie, an affable, heavyset, older man, asked, "Luke, did you meet Mickey?" when Luke answered, Charlie said, "You know, he's a jockey."

Something clicked in Luke's mind: "They are like royalty.... They make lots of money." That's how Jacinto described jockeys the time he took Luke to the racetrack months earlier. Suddenly, in his young mind, Luke imagined Mickey as a rich guy, driving a new Cadillac and with many pretty girlfriends.

He went back out, sat next to Jose and listened to the two brothers talking, happy to see each other. As Mickey spoke, Luke couldn't help noticing the diamond wristwatch and the equally expensive looking monogrammed gold bracelet. While he didn't much care for jewelry, it reinforced Luke's notion that jockeys made a lot of money.

One of the waiters called an order and Jose got up and said to his brother, "I'll be right back; talk to Luke."

Luke spoke first, "I heard you're a jockey."

Mickey answered, "Yes. I'm here for the Lincoln Downs meeting that starts next week. I'll ride there until it's time to go back to West Virginia in the spring." He continued, "Do you go to school?"

"Yap," answered Luke, quickly changing the conversation back to the racetrack, "I went to Lincoln Downs last year for the first time. I'd like to work there." And with all the courage he could muster, the youngster asked, "Can you help me get a job like yours?"

A half hour later, Mickey got up to leave. Again, the brothers hugged each other. Jose mentioned dinner once his brother got settled. Luke shook Mickey's hand again and said, "Glad to meet you. Don't forget what I said about the job."

"I'll see what I can do," Mickey said smiling as he walked out the door waving goodbye.

Back at work, as he loaded the dishwasher, Luke said, "Jose, I didn't know you had a brother who is a jockey."

"You know how it is Luke," Jose said. "He's traveling all the time, and we don't get to see each other much."

For the rest of the evening and the next day all Luke could think about was Mickey getting him a job as a jockey.

5

A month went by without hearing a word from Mickey Gomez. After giving it a lot of thought, he decided to go to Lincoln Downs himself. The bus terminal was on the plaza across from O'Rourke's, and days earlier, already thinking it may come to this, Luke asked the clerk in the ticket booth for a schedule of the bus from Providence to the town of Lincoln, where the racetrack was located.

The first bus left the station daily at 5:30 a.m. If he was going to take the bus, he'd need to think of an excuse to tell his mother why he was leaving the house so early.

Since starting to work at O'Rourke's, it was part of Luke's job to clean the front glass windows and door of the restaurant every Saturday morning. He usually started the window cleaning job at about 9:00 a.m. Luke thought he'd tell his mother that they wanted him to do the windows before Saturday, and since it was a weekday, he had to start earlier.

"What about school?" his mother asked.

"Oh, it doesn't take that long," he said, "I will be back in time for class." The anticipation of going to the racetrack did little to erase the bad feeling of not telling his mother the truth.

The bus left the station promptly at 5:30 in the morning while it was still dark out. The ride took 35 minutes. Aside from Luke, there was only one other passenger on the bus wearing work clothes and holding a large portable radio. Luke wondered if the man was going to the track, too. The bus stop was across the street from a little coffee house outside the Lincoln Downs parking lot. Luke crossed the street with the other passenger behind him. With no idea where to go to apply for a job, he turned to the man and asked, "Excuse me, where do you go for jobs?"

"HR is through that first set of doors," the man said, pointing ahead to the grandstand building, "Follow me."

Upon entering the building, once again the man pointed to the HR office as he turned to go in the opposite direction. Luke walked through the double doors and found himself in a large office where a woman sat at a desk shuffling file folders. He walked up to the counter.

"May I help you?" asked the clerk looking over the rim of her glasses.

"Yes. I'd like to apply for a job, please."

"Certainly," she said and proceeded to hand Luke an application, "Just fill this out. By the way, how old are you?"

Without a second thought, he said, "Eighteen." Hoping he wouldn't be asked for I.D.

"You look like just a boy," she said smiling.

One of the questions on the application inquired what position the applicant was interested in. Luke wrote "jockey." When the clerk came back, Luke handed her the completed application. She scanned the information, and when she came to the "position required" line, she looked at Luke and said, "You're applying to be a jockey? You don't do that here; we have nothing to do with that."

Confused, Luke asked, "Where do I go then?"

With an annoyed tone, the woman said, "I don't know what to tell you. You may want to see the stewards in the backside."

Luke thanked the clerk and exited the building. He was totally confused, "Stewards? Backside? What the heck is that?" For a moment, he stood there. He pulled out the bus schedule from his pocket. The next bus going back to the city was at 8:30 a.m. While thinking what to do, he looked across the parking lot and through a chain link fence saw the barns where Jacinto Hernandez had taken him many months before. He got closer to the fence and saw people working with the horses. Steam released from the bodies of some of the horses as men used buckets of warm water to wash them down. He stood there taking it all in when a security guard called from the door of a small shack a short distance away.

"What are you doing kid? You looking for somebody?"

The answer was instant. It came to him from nowhere, "Yes. I'm here to see my friend Jacinto Hernandez. He's a groom."

Jacinto was on his knees in a stall wrapping white cotton bandages on the front legs of a horse when he heard his name over the loudspeaker. He had a visitor at the guard gate. *Who the heck could that be?* he thought to himself. "Boss, I'll be right back," he called out to trainer Buddy Hanes sitting on his stable pony outside the barn.

"Hey, my gringito, what are you doing here?" Jacinto said, smiling at the sight of Luke on the other side of the fence. As the gate was opened for Luke to enter, in his signature broken English, Jacinto said to the guard, "This boy's going to be a great rider someday. If Shoe make it, he make it!" The time would come when Luke would know what Jacinto meant by the quip.

At the barn, Jacinto showed him how to hold the leather strap clipped to the halter, and walked the horse around the shedrow with Luke until he got the hang of it after one turn around the barn. "Let him have a couple of sips of water from this bucket every other turn," Jacinto told him, pointing at a bucket on top of a stool.

That morning, Hanes hired Luke to be a hot walker. It was up to Luke to think of what to tell his mother.

He was ready to leave the racetrack by 1:00 p.m. Chores were all finished at the barn until feeding time later in the afternoon; Luke was not required to be there. Jacinto drove him home. Although the youngster said he'd take the bus back, Jacinto wouldn't hear of it.

Luke still hadn't figured what to tell his mother, even though in his mind the decision was made. She would not be home until after five p.m., and he had to be at the restaurant at 4:00. Never mind that he had skipped school that day.

He showered, had a bite to eat and started the walk downtown. Things were quiet at O'Rourke's until the dinner crowd started to arrive around six o'clock. Jose and Charlie were sitting reading the newspaper in a rear booth. As Luke walked toward them, he said hello and sat down.

"Jose, there's something I need to talk to you about," Luke said.

Charlie put down the sports page he was reading and said, "If it's private I can leave."

Luke looked at the chef and said, "No, you can stay. You'll find out eventually anyway."

Luke told Jose what he had done that day and the decision he had made. He said he was sorry if this was going to cause trouble for Jose with the restaurant's manager. After all, the reason he was hired was the result of Jose's recommendation. Both men listened to Luke without saying a word.

After a moment of silence, Jose said, "Luke, I've heard everything you've said. What I haven't heard is how you are planning to handle your mother. What is she going to say about this? What about school?" At that point, Charlie got up and said he'd be in the kitchen.

"Honestly Jose, I haven't got that far yet." He continued, "I wanted to talk to you first. I wanted to hear your opinion."

"Luke, your mother and I have spoken about you more than once." He played with his eyeglasses on the table as he spoke, "Her dream has always been that you finish school and go to college. You have a knack for drawing and painting." He went on, "You've told me more than once you wanted to be an artist. Frankly, I think this racetrack thing is going to break her heart." Jose continued, "This jockey business is not as glamorous as it seems. Many times my brother has struggled to find mounts; he's been seriously hurt more than once. The thing is, he can't do anything else. He never finished school."

Luke looked over to see the dinner customers starting to come in. Luke and Jose went back in the kitchen without any more discussion.

His mother was doing a load of laundry when he got home later that night. "I'm back here, Luke."

He walked back to the pantry, gave her a kiss, and said, "Mom, I need to talk to you." Things went downhill from there.

Luke explained, but she wouldn't listen. "This is absolutely not acceptable; I can't believe you'd think I'd go along with this," she said in a loud voice.

Aunt Lucy walked in the door, went to the kitchen and said, "What's going on here? I could hear you all the way up the stairs."

Eleven o'clock and nothing had been resolved. Luke got ready for bed, sure that he wouldn't go back to the racetrack the next day. What he did know is that he wanted to be a jockey, no matter what.

The two women went in the living room and continued talking about Luke after putting away the dishes.

Lucy Morales was the older of the two sisters. Her husband had passed away several years before due to complications from heart surgery. Eventually, she moved out of her apartment and came to live with her sister and nephew. She was like a second mother to Luke; in many ways, he could talk to her easier than to his mother.

Lucy was also a pragmatist. "Luke has less than two years left of high school. What do you think about letting him give this racetrack job a try and go to night school? I'm sure he'll agree. By the time he graduates, he may change his mind anyway. If not," she said with a smile, "Who knows, maybe someday we'll go to the Kentucky Derby."

The next day Luke went to school, and later back to his shift at the restaurant. After all, he hadn't officially quit the job at O'Rourke's. Before leaving the house, he called the racetrack and left a message for Jacinto, that he would not be coming back and thanked him for everything. "Tell him I still owe him that beer," he said to the guard at the other end of the phone. As much as he wanted to go against his mother, Luke knew that in the end, he couldn't hurt her.

That evening when Luke returned from work, his mother and his aunt were sitting around the dining room table. "Sit down, Luke," his aunt said, "We need to talk to you." They set out the plan that Aunt Lucy had come up with the night before. Tears welled in Luke's eyes as he quickly agreed to night school. He was going back to Lincoln Downs after all, this time with his mother's consent.

6

With his mother's approval for what she hoped would be a temporary racetrack career, there were several things Luke needed to do the following day.

First, he called the racetrack and left a message for Jacinto: "Things have changed at home. I can come back to work for Mr. Hanes in a couple days if the job is still available." After telling Jose what had happened with his mother, he went to the owner, Mr. O'Rourke, to thank him for giving him the opportunity to work at the restaurant. He told the boss that he would stay on long enough for a replacement to be hired.

"Don't worry about that Luke. We'll handle it. We just want to wish you good luck. We enjoyed having you here. Come by and see us anytime," said Mr. O'Rourke patting the youngster on the back.

He enrolled in a night high school program offered by the local community college due to start at the end of June, a month and a half away. While his present school was four blocks away from home, he'd rely on public transportation to get to and from the new school.

Four nights after the conversation with his mother and Aunt Lucy, Luke set his alarm for 4:45 a.m., got his working clothes ready and went to bed at 10:00 p.m. to get up early and catch the downtown bus to begin what he knew would be an exciting riding career.

His weekly salary working for horse trainer Hanes was $25 and some change after taxes. The track kitchen, more like a cafeteria, offered a weekly meal ticket for six dollars and 50 cents, which included a light breakfast and a sandwich lunch for five days. With the nearest places to eat a distance away in town, most track employees took advantage of the meal ticket.

Luke kept busy raking the shedrow, fetching water buckets or helping the grooms while waiting for horses to return from their daily exercise at the track. Once back, the hot horse would be held in place by Luke or one of the other two hot walkers while the groom bathed the animal. Once done, the horse was walked 25 to 45 minutes, depending on how fast the exercise, until it was cooled down and dry before returning it to the stall.

Lincoln Downs was one of two racetracks in Rhode Island. The other, Narragansett Park, was located across town in the city of Pawtucket, close to the border with Massachusetts. Each track operated during the same months every other year: one year Lincoln, the next year Gansett. Because they were open during the worst months of the year—fall and winter—their seasons were longer than the other New England tracks, which operated during the spring and summer. Their seasons started within a couple of days after the conclusion of racing at the Rhode Island tracks.

Boston's Suffolk Downs was next on the racing schedule followed by New Hampshire's Rockingham Park in the summer. The latter two showcased the best racing of the circuit. Counting other smaller operations in Vermont and Maine, plus the Massachusetts summer county fairs, thoroughbred and harness racing was a thriving year-round industry in the northeast corner of the country, employing hundreds of people. The picture changed during the 1970s and later years, as horse racing in New England became a victim of the new state lotteries and casinos later on.

But for Luke, that was enough time. During the ensuing months, he changed jobs three times, each time for a couple of dollars more and better promises of teaching him to ride. With the advent of spring, racing switched to Suffolk Downs. A couple of Luke's friends, also aspiring jockeys, worked for the large stable of one of the perennial leading trainers in New England, David Raymond, who due to the large number of horses he trained, was always on the lookout for more help. His friends introduced Luke to the tall, thin, young man who was Raymond's assistant.

Vince Muller hoped to be a jockey during his early teens, but as he continued to grow in size the chance for him to ride races went from remote to impossible, he opted instead to become a trainer someday. At nearly six feet tall, his slender frame still allowed him to be a premier exercise rider. Aside from supervising the Raymond stable, he was also its chief exercise boy along with four others. Some of the other exercise boys were ex-jockeys who had become too heavy to continue their race riding careers. When it became time for horses to work—a faster form of exercising—jockeys came around the barn willing to do the chore for free in the hope of riding the horses in races, where the money was.

Raymond would be the last trainer to employ Luke before he became a jockey. Vince Muller liked the teenager well enough to hire him as a hot walker with the promise he'd teach him to gallop horses. That he didn't speak broken English, like most of the other employees of the Raymond stable, was an advantage. With his desire to learn everything about racehorses, in time, Luke became Muller's favorite hire.

7

Although Lincoln Downs and Narraganset Park also operated in winter, Maryland's Bowie Race Course, named after the town where it was located, was the only racetrack on the East Coast to offer lucrative stakes and major races other than Florida during that time of the year. Hosting top flight trainers, jockeys and horses, it was the alternative for horsemen who, for some reason or another, opted not to go to sunny Miami or Tampa for the winter.

The Bowie stable area was divided into three sites. The largest, known as Queenstown, faced Racetrack Road across the street from the racing strip's backstretch. Until a bridge was built over the county road years later, a crossing guard stopped traffic as horses crossed the paved road on their way to and from the track. Next was Blueberry Hill, a slope high atop the same county road where several barns were located. A dirt path through the woods rising from the area of the far turn allowed horses stabled there access to the racetrack.

The third, simply referred to as "back of the grandstand," was a small area closest to the grandstand building with a couple of barns generally occupied by the same trainers each year.

For Luke, it was the first time he had ever been away from home by himself. More and more, his mother was making peace with the reality that horse racing was going to be her son's chosen career, especially now that by following the stable to Maryland, he failed to finish high school, although he promised to do so when he returned home in the spring.

Upon arrival at Bowie, dorm rooms for the help were assigned by Muller, two employees to a room. Luke was going to bunk with the same teenager he had ridden with in the back of the horse van for the trip from Rhode Island. A year behind Luke in experience and roughly of the same age, Tom Sweeny, unlike Luke, was a streetwise kid. The first time they met at Rockingham the previous summer, with a cigarette hanging from his lips, Tom wore a Hell's Angels leather jacket that was way too big for such a small kid. He was accompanied by two other taller teenagers and a heavyset girl that Luke supposed was the moll of the gang. The four had jumped the fence that ran along the backroad of the stable area across from the Raymond barn.

The little gang hung around for a while that morning watching the goings on at the barn. It was the first time any of them had seen horses up close.

Several days later, on a trip to the track kitchen, Luke was approached by Sweeny, now wearing a less threatening windbreaker, and asked, "You think I can get a job where you work?"

By the time they reached Bowie they had become good friends. In the afternoons, once all the work was done at the barn, they'd go to the races and search trash barrels looking for a program that someone may have discarded to read the names of horses and jockeys in each race. Eventually, along with the found program, Tom would pilfer a Racing Form from an unsuspecting bettor so they could try their hands at handicapping.

As the days went by they met other teenagers working for other trainers also aspiring to be jockeys. Some were already galloping horses. The group would go to the races, each putting up 50 cents or a dollar to bet a race. After several unsuccessful bets, they decided to concentrate their efforts on the feature race each day, where better horses had the propensity to run truer to their past performances. Whenever they were unable to pool the six dollars for a combination ticket that would pay off if their selection finished first, second or third, they would play it safe and just bet a show ticket on the horse of their choice.

But, of course, at that rate they never hit big. Once the race winnings were shared, each boy would have a net profit of a dollar or less.

Luke and Tom's salaries came to $28 cash each after taxes. Every payday evening the older employees would clean up, don their best change of clothes and blow most of their salaries at a little bar in the old town of Bowie that offered music from a jukebox and the odd girl here and there to dance with. The next day they would be hung over and broke but laughing that none of them ever got past first base with the bar's girls.

Not being old enough to go along to the bar, instead, Luke and Tom would hustle a ride to town. Luke would wire $15 to his mother, buy a 10-dollar meal ticket at the track kitchen (breakfasts, lunches and dinners for a week), and keep three dollars for himself. Tom, on the other hand, would con someone to buy him a bottle of cheap whiskey and lure three stable hands into a game of poker in Luke and Tom's room in the bunk house.

Each room consisted of enough space for two folding cots. The boys' room also had a little black and white TV with a makeshift wire clothes hanger for an antenna that Luke had brought from home. It sat on top of a built-in cabinet in a corner of the small room.

Shortly after arriving at Bowie, Tom picked up a piece of wood someone had discarded in a manure pile. He washed it off, and painted it white from a small can of paint Muller kept in the tack room. The Friday night card table consisted of the piece of wood on top of an upside-down metal water bucket. Tom and the other three would sit on the floor around the "table." Tom would open the bottle of bad whiskey and pass it around for his marks to each take a sip. When it came back around, Tom would make believe he too took a hit and quickly passed the bottle to the next guy. As the night wore on and with the others half-drunk, Tom would cheat them out of most of their pay every week. All the while, on the bed watching TV, Luke feared the men would catch Tom dealing from the bottom of the deck one night, and he too would suffer the consequences of Tom's cheating.

By midweek, Luke's three dollars were usually spent on sweet treats from the track kitchen. He resorted to borrowing a dollar or two from Tom to bet the races, which was really their only pastime. Of course, Tom always had more than enough money from his salary plus his weekend enterprise; he never bothered asking Luke to pay him back.

Each Sunday night, Luke would call his mother collect from a phone booth near the bunkhouse in Blueberry Hill. He would tell his mother about all the things he was learning, and how much he enjoyed Bowie. He never dared mention how much he missed being home." Son, I don't like you being so far away," she'd say. "Why don't you come home?"

On Thanksgiving Day, the local horsemen's association sponsored a dinner in the track kitchen for all the employees. Although alcoholic beverages were not allowed, some grooms sipped from pint bottles hidden inside their coats. That night, walking back to his room with Tom, Luke silently thought how much he missed being home for the holidays.

Wednesday was draw day at the Raymond barn. Employees who wished an advance from their weekly salary would be fronted 10 or 20 dollars. The Wednesday before Christmas, Luke asked Mr. Raymond if he would mind very much if he flew home on Christmas Eve and came back to work the day after Christmas. When Raymond agreed, the hard part came of asking if he could front Luke the $75 it would cost for the roundtrip airplane ticket from Baltimore to Providence.

Sitting down at his desk in the tack room, Raymond cast a look at Luke while thinking about the request. He had made similar deals with other employees over the years, and he knew how unreliable some racetrack workers could be: they'd tell you they were coming back and next thing you know the trainer would be out the front money and looking for someone to take their place. But this boy was a different case, the trainer finally decided.

"I'll tell you what. I'll give you the money for the airplane and deduct it from your first four paychecks after that." Before Luke could speak, the trainer said, "On those four paydays I'll just give enough for a meal ticket."

Good thing Tom will be around when I get back, Luke thought.

Luke was home on the afternoon of Christmas Eve. His mother had the Christmas tree all lighted up in the living room of their apartment, with several boxes wrapped in colorful paper on the floor under the tree. The next day, Luke opened his presents, mostly warm socks and underwear he could take back with him. Later, with his grandparents, Aunt Lucy, and Jose also sitting at the table, they had the great meal his mother always served during holidays. Everyone asking Luke how things were going at the racetrack.

That evening, his mother and Aunt Lucy drove him back to the airport, both of them with tears in their eyes as they saw him off. Once seated in the airplane, Luke's own sadness was obvious.

PART TWO

As agreed, Vince Muller picked Luke up at the airport in Baltimore at 9:30 Christmas night. When he dropped him off late morning the day before, they had settled that Luke would stay overnight at Vince's place upon his return, and drive to the track together the next morning.

Driving to the apartment in suburban Lanham and sharing how each other had spent their short Christmas, Vince told Luke that Tom had gone back to Providence. "It took me by surprise," said Vince. "He caught a ride this morning on a van with a load of horses going to Narragansett," he continued, "I thought he was happy here."

"Yeah, me too," said Luke.

"He'll never get to ride races pulling shit like that. I'd told him I would start him on horses before long," said Vince dropping the subject.

On the third day of the New Year, three new horses arrived from a training center in New Jersey to join the Raymond stable. One of them was a scrawny gray filly by the name of *Sweet Song*. Vince didn't know if the horse was naturally that skinny or if she just hadn't been fed enough. They had the stable's veterinarian run blood and fecal tests on the new arrivals and check their overall health. For the next three days, the only exercise those three got was walking around the shed for 45 minutes.

On the fourth day, Raymond scheduled *Sweet Song* for a light one-mile gallop to go out with the first set of five horses to the track that morning. Vince put the outfit's lightest exercise boy on her, a middle-aged Mexican by the name of Marcelo. He had been a jockey in Southern California many years earlier and was experienced enough to judge the ability of horses he got on, something that was of great help to the trainer.

When the horses returned from the track, Luke stood by the filly's stall waiting for the groom to put the halter back on after Marcelo took off the saddle and bridle. Once haltered, Luke ran the lead shank through the left brass loop of the halter, over her nose and snapped it on the other side. Walking toward the stall from the stable office, Vince yelled to the grooms, "No baths today! It's too chilly this morning; just rub them down." As he engaged Marcelo in front of *Sweet Song*'s stall, Vince asked, "How did she go?"

In his broken English, the exercise rider said, "No too bad boss; she little even for me. She no take a hold o' nothing."

Again, the filly was scheduled to gallop the following morning. Arriving at the barn earlier than usual, Vince was by a stall speaking to the groom brushing the horse. He called Luke, and asked, "Do you have galloping boots?"

Luke didn't know why Vince would ask that, but answered, "No, sir."

"Follow me to the tack room, will you."

As Luke entered the room, Vince said, "Sit down on the chair. I'm going to wrap these bandages around your legs." Luke felt a rush as his heart started thumping out of his chest. He had seen guys without boots gallop horses with their legs wrapped with bandages to keep them from chafing.

"Grab that helmet on the wall and come with me," said Vince, "You're going to get on the gray filly; I'll go beside you on the pony." They walked down to the stall, Vince said, "Now grab the reins with your left hand, put the right hand on top of the saddle and boost yourself up when I give you a leg up." It was the only time Vince would need to tell Luke how to get on a horse.

Once on the way to the track, Vince told Luke how to tie and hold the reins, tighten the girth and how to adjust his stirrups. He explained how keeping his left stirrup longer than the right helped maintain better balance around the turns. Slowly, Vince's pony started to trot, and in rhythm with the horses, the riders sat up and down from their knees, *posting* in prelude to a gallop.

They went once around the mile oval. Upon pulling up, Vince asked, "How do you feel, Luke, tired?"

Although winded, Luke was in heaven. He couldn't believe he had finally ridden a race horse.

9

Over the next few months, starting off with the gray filly, Vince made it a practice to let Luke get on the easiest horses early in the morning, before Raymond arrived. The assistant didn't know how the boss would react if he knew that Luke was getting on horses without his knowledge.

As the Bowie meeting was coming to an end later that winter, three horses were saddled ready to go the racetrack to breeze together. Two jockeys were standing by already waiting for the third rider to arrive. Raymond was nervous. It was shortly before 10:00 a.m., the time when the racetrack normally closed for training.

"Vince, tell Marcelo to get on that third horse. Let's go. We have to make the racetrack."

"Marcelo left a little while ago, Dave."

"Jesus Christ, you're going to have to get on the horse yourself," the annoyed Raymond cursed.

"Dave, Luke can work that horse," said Vince.

"Luke?" exclaimed Raymond mounting the stable pony.

"Dave, I've been taking him to the racetrack for a while. He can work the horse."

"Well, let's go. Hurry up," the trainer said, shaking his head.
Vince yelled at Luke, who had just finished walking a horse, "Get your helmet. You've got a horse to work!"

Luke ran to the tack room for the helmet. Weeks before, he had stopped sending his mother the $15 from his pay until he had enough to buy a new pair of galloping boots from the manufacturer in the town of Laurel.

With the two jockeys already mounted and on the way to the track, Vince gave Luke a leg up, and said, "Remember what you've learned, buddy."

The three horses broke together just before the half-mile pole and finished noses apart at the wire.

Upon returning to the barn, Raymond told Vince, "The kid did well." For Luke, it was the thrill of a lifetime.

Shortly after that, Luke began getting on tougher horses, and within weeks learned how to break from the starting gate getting instruction from the same two jockeys.

10

It was May, and the Raymond outfit had already settled down at their Suffolk Downs headquarters ready to start the spring meet. After breaking from the starting gate several more times and able to gallop virtually any horse, it had been decided that Raymond would take out an apprentice contract on Luke to start the teenager's career as the stable's jockey. As an apprentice, Luke would receive a weight allowance of five pounds meaning that his mounts would have the advantage of carrying less weight than other horses in the race during the time of the apprenticeship.

The day came when Luke took the standard three-year contract home for his mother to sign. He was two weeks short of his eighteenth birthday. The document spelled out the conditions of the arrangement with David Raymond. Aside from receiving the $27 riding fee and a percentage of the money earned by his mounts, Raymond would pay him $250 dollars per month for the first year. The yearly increases thereafter would net $450 monthly for the third year.

The next day, Raymond drove Luke to meet the stewards and make the contract official.

A month later, Raymond scheduled Luke to ride two races on a weekday card. On the way to the starting gate on his first mount, he remembered Jacinto Hernandez saying, "If Shoe make it, you make it," over two years before. The groom was referring to top jockey, William Shoemaker, who many called by the nickname of Shoe, and Luke making it like the champion rider.

"Good luck, Luke," said Vince from aboard the lead pony as he handed the horse to the assistant starter.

Once loaded into the gate, the handler settling the horse said, "Sit still Luke. We're going to get you out of here in front." Short minutes went by as two other horses were loaded. Suddenly, the bell rang as the doors opened and Luke was riding his first race.

That both his mounts that day finished off the board was of no consequence; they were long-shots meant to give Luke some experience. Luke used the occasions to practice switching his whip from one hand to the other the way he had seen top jockeys do in Maryland.

For a long time, Luke had noticed attractive girls hanging around the entrance to the jockeys' room. While some of them were wives waiting for their jockey husbands, others were just hoping to catch the eye of a rider. Luke knew his time had come when two such girls ran up and asked for his autograph as he exited the jockeys' quarters after riding that afternoon.

One morning, as Luke entered the barn after getting up from his bed in the bunkroom he now shared with Vince, he saw Tom Sweeny hanging around by the office tack room speaking to one of the grooms.

"What do you say, Luke?" Tom called out. "You got that money you owe me?" he said laughing.

They shook hands and Luke said "Man, you left Bowie like it was *you* who owed somebody money. How come?"

"I met a trainer that was shipping to Gansett and offered me a job for a few more bucks." He continued, "Eventually, he let me gallop horses, and is ready to put me on a contract so I can start riding races."

"That's great Tom. Sounds like you have your nose to the grindstone and are staying out of trouble."

"Ah, it's trouble that finds me; you know that." They both laughed.

While the Raymond stable had started winning races at its usual clip with other jockeys riding over the next several months, Luke was only allowed to ride a few more races aboard horses with no real shot at winning. Raymond's plan was to have Luke gain plenty of experience so once he started riding live mounts the following spring he'd be able to successfully compete against veteran riders. The trainer was looking out for Luke's best interest.

Back at Lincoln Downs later that year, an exercise rider friend of Luke's convinced his employer to give Luke a shot on a small bay filly that had been racing poorly. "Why not take the weight off and ride an apprentice?" the youngster reasoned to his boss.

The following week Luke read the overnight—the list of entries for the following racing day—and saw his name next to a horse whose name he didn't recognize. Before he could find out who the trainer of the horse was, his friend Lonnie came to the Raymond barn looking for Luke.

"Hey, you see my boss put you on a horse tomorrow?"

"Hi, Lonnie. I was wondering whose horse that was," Luke replied.

"She's going to run good, Luke. She's in the right spot, "Lonnie said, "She's been running against tougher company."

The filly named *Time's Right* was the first horse Luke would ride for someone other than the Raymond stable. In the paddock the next day, speaking with a Midwestern drawl, the trainer said to Luke with a smile, "Well, Lonnie says you're a hell of a rider, so let's see if he's right. She's easy enough to ride, has a little speed; use it if you can. As they say back home, goodbye starter, hello judge," quipped the smiling trainer.

It had rained earlier that morning; the best place to be on a sloppy track was in the lead, or near it. Breaking from the number two stall, Luke sent the horse at the start and quickly went to the front of seven rivals. The filly widened her lead around the turn, began to lag a little through the stretch and after Luke tapped her a few times with his whip, the horse lasted to win by a length and half.

Upon returning to the winner's circle, Lonnie walked out onto the muddy racetrack to meet Luke aboard the horse, and after clamping the lead shank on the bridle, he said "My man!" and slapped Luke's hand, both smiling broadly.

Standing by to watch the race, Vince Muller quickly ran down and also posed for the winner's circle photo. Upon dismounting, Luke shook the hand of the filly's trainer and thanked him for allowing him to ride her.

"Heck, Lonnie would have quit me if I had put someone else on her," the affable trainer said smiling.

The ritual is very amusing, but it can also be somewhat cruel. When Luke entered the jockeys' room after winning the race, one jockey soaked him with a bucket of ice water, as two other riders wrestled him to the floor pulling down his pants, a fourth one painted Luke's body with black shoe polish, with special attention to the genitals. Everyone else laughed and got out of the way. Luke had broken his maiden! He had ridden his first winner. A newspaper man and a photographer stood by recording the event.

The next morning, the usually taciturn Raymond waited until Luke and all the exercise riders were mounted on their horses. On the way to the track, he tapped Luke's booted leg, and said "Congratulations," although he was disappointed that Luke didn't ride his first winner on a horse trained by him.

As usual, Bowie again was the stable's winter quarters. Three weeks into the meet, Raymond called Luke into the tack room one morning. "Luke, I'm thinking of sending five horses back to Lincoln with you and a groom. These horses won't do against the tougher company down here. Anyway, you'll get to ride the five. *Golden Eagle* will be one of them." Golden Eagle was a seven-year-old gelding that had been a stakes winner at three and four and whose ability was slowly diminishing with age. He would be the best horse Luke would ride to date.

Several days later, back in Providence, Luke was glad to be home. He remembered how lonesome Maryland was. His Aunt Lucy would drop him off at the track each morning on her way to work, and he'd get a ride back home from a groom that lived in the projects not far from Luke's apartment.

By the end of the Lincoln Downs meeting, Luke had won another eight races. All of Raymond's trainees had won at least once, and also rode winners for other trainers.

In particular, a non-winning mount was trained by a Puerto Rican trainer stabled one barn over from the Raymond horses. His name was Isael Martinez, but everybody called him by his nickname, *Crazy Issy*. He was well-known for winning most of his races each summer at the Massachusetts fair circuit with a modest string of bottom rung claimers. He was boastful and loud, always having something outrageous to say in his broken English.

Several years earlier, Martinez had trained a horse named *Taylor's Hope*, which won five races in eight days at one of the fairs. When the local SPCA came to investigate what seemed cruel treatment, Martinez told them "I run *Taylor* a short distance, five furlongs, no more, on a nice even track with a little jockey on his back," he said. "This Paul Revere, he's a hero around here, rode his horse 26 miles at full speed in one night on a dirt road!"

One morning, Martinez approached Luke in the track kitchen and told him he had a horse for him to ride. "I put him in for Wednesday." Luke thanked the trainer and asked him if he needed him to come by to get on the horse, to which the trainer said, "No, is all right."

On the day of the race, Luke walked in the paddock, and he saw his mount, *Lucky Lou*, puffing, huffing and refusing to stand still, rearing up and kicking as his groom tried to hold him in place while Martinez and the valet attempted to put the saddle on the lunging animal. Once saddled, the horse dragged the poor handler as they made a round in the walking ring.

To his young jockey, the trainer said, "Don't worry about the 99 to 1 odds, jock. This horse can't read." Serious as a heart attack, he told Luke to let him come out of the gate and go right to the lead.

Lucky Lou was number eight in a field of as many horses. Lincoln Downs was less than a mile in circumference. This meant at seven furlongs the starting gate was stationed in front of the grandstand. Still puffing and now drenched in sweat, the horse tried to climb over the lead pony several times with Luke bouncing off the saddle and holding onto the horse's mane.

It took three assistant starters to load *Lou* in the gate. Finally, inside the stall, an assistant held down the horse's tail while another one did all he could do to keep the horse in place. As the gates sprang open, the horse quickly charged toward the outer rail, with Luke pulling on the reins unable to control the horse. Still running at full speed along the outside fence around the turn, the outrider came to the aid and pulled up Luke and his mount, holding the horse in place until the race was over to lead them back to the unsaddling area.

As the groom took hold of the horse's swinging head while Luke unsaddled the animal, Martinez rushed toward Luke shouting, "Damned jockeys, no matter how young they are they still no let the horse run!"

Undoing the saddle and proceeding to the scale, Luke walked toward the jockeys' room with his head down disgusted at the circus his mount and the trainer had caused in front of the crowd. As he reached the door, he felt Martinez' arm on his shoulders saying, "Sorry about what I said back there, jock. I told the owner the horse couldn't lose, and he bet his money." He continued, "But I knew maybe he wasn't going to run well. You see, I bought him a week ago for $500 dollars from a trainer that feed him good, kept him comfortable in a stall bedded down with nice straw, but the horse never run a lick." Then came the kicker: "Anyway, I thought I change a few things around and see if I had any luck with the sonofabitch, so I let him sleep on the dirt floor, and fed him just hay and water for the last four days!"

Luke made it a point never to ride for Martinez again.

PART THREE

When the rest of the Raymond outfit shipped back north at the start of Suffolk Downs in April, the trainer approached a jockey's agent he had known for many years. The veteran Paul Dwyer represented one of New England's top jockeys, Bob Tracy, during the rider's entire career of 30-plus-years, but was now on the verge of retiring from riding. In fact, the same jockey had been the Raymond stable jockey in the early days.

"Paul, I've got this young Cuban boy," Raymond began.

"You mean Nodarse? I've been watching him," said Dwyer.

"With Tracy retiring, I'd like you to take his book and handle his business."

"You know a good bug boy is always a hot commodity around here." (Apprentice jockeys are commonly called bug boys because of the asterisk next to their weight in the racing program.) The agent, continued, "As I said, I've been watching him. Why, he has a mean left hand when whipping a horse on that side."

"You're right," Raymond replied with a smile, "Anyway, he's a good kid, a hard worker. Talk to him will you?"

"Don't worry Dave; I'll take good care of him."

With Dwyer as his agent and the Raymond horses winning at a fast clip, by June of that year, Luke had ridden a total of 24 winners including two minor stakes races. At this point, he was the leading jockey at the meet and the toast of the town. Eight thousand dollar in less than two months was a lot of money for most people in the mid-1960s. Luke, had just turned 19 years of age and was on top of the world.

The first thing he did was buy a car. Dwyer introduced him to a friend who owned a dealership. The car man was a regular at the races and liked to bet on Luke's mounts. Several days later the agent drove the young jockey to the car lot, and the owner gave him an excellent deal on a new two-door Buick Skylark.

Then came the day when, after riding the winners of the first and third races, Luke was injured as the first of three jockeys who went down in a spill in the seventh race.

12

It had been five weeks since the spill, and his fractured ribs were feeling better. His right leg was also coming along under a now shorter cast, and he could get around easily with the aid of crutches. He used the prescribed pain medicine only a couple of times during the first week after coming home from the hospital. Since then, an aspirin here and there. His mother had always waited on him hand and foot, but the spill had taken it to the max: his favorite meals, the best desserts and the TV's remote control readily at hand while sitting in the recliner.

But she needed a little rest, plus Luke was growing antsy by the minute. It seemed Aunt Lucy worked later and later, and would come home only to eat and sleep. The schedule kept her from being any help with Luke.

One evening, confident that he could get around better than he was, his mother asked, "Isn't Lincoln Downs racing nights now?"

"Yeah, they're making up for all the cancellations they had last winter," he answered.

"Luke, you should call a friend to take you out there. You know, get out of the house for a while; see people."

After thinking about it for several minutes, he said, "Mom, if I were to go out there, I could drive myself."

"With a cast on your leg?" she exclaimed.

"Hey mom, you should know your son has many talents; I can use my left foot to work the pedals." He chuckled.

Despite his mother's apprehension about Luke driving with only one foot, an hour later he was on his way to the racetrack.

Everyone in the jockeys' room was glad to see Luke. He sat by his locker speaking to Cosmo, his valet, who aside from taking care of Luke's equipment, also looked out for him like an older brother.

Luke stayed for four races. As he was getting up to leave, Cosmo came back from saddling a horse for the next race and said to him, "Hey, Karen is outside. I told her you were here. She wants to say hi."

Karen was trouble . . . good trouble. Luke had met her months before when leaving the apartment he rented across from the beach near Suffolk Downs when riding there. They never really dated, but still, she showed the inexperienced Luke pleasures he never imagined.

"See you, Cos; maybe I'll be whole in a couple of weeks," he said to his valet as he managed the door of the jockeys' quarters.

Karen ran up and kissed his lips, not passionately, but certainly more than just as a casual acquaintance.

"How are you doing? Getting better?"

"Just going along." Luke couldn't deny he was happy to see her.

"Here, let me introduce you to my boss, April." Shortly after meeting Luke the previous year, the voluptuous Karen gave up her job at a mortgage brokerage office and came to work at the track as a hot walker. But Luke never knew who Karen worked for.

The trainer was older than Karen, maybe early 30s. She had long black hair done in a ponytail; her pretty face accentuated by green eyes and a few freckles. She shook his hand with a smile. "Karen has told me about you," she said smiling.

"Really? What did she tell you, that I'm good at falling off horses?" he quipped.

"Among other things," she replied with a smile and the wink of an eye.

An excited Karen said, "Why don't you follow us home? I live at April's. We'll have a drink."

Previous nights with Karen flashed in Luke's mind. He decided neither sensitive ribs nor a leg in a cast could stand in the way of a Karen instant replay.

The drive was almost an hour. They turned into the tree-lined driveway of what seemed a mansion to Luke. The lighted front porch featured tall Federal style columns that led to a set of large double doors that opened to a beautifully appointed foyer and into the living room.

This April must come from real money, Luke thought to himself. *What's she doing training horses?*

"Karen, get Luke a drink. I need to take care of the babysitter," April called as she walked to the other end of the house.

As Karen fixed the drink at a bar by the hallway door to the pool yard, Luke was left alone in the spacious living room. Everything looked expensive, the furniture, the drapes covering the large picture windows, a shiny black piano in a far corner.

Several framed photographs were placed here and there. It called Luke's attention that all of them were not only in black and white, but the subjects were all the same: Men leaning on expensive automobiles or sitting around tables. One in particular, reminiscent of a gangster movie, was of three men leaning against a wall wearing fedoras and long overcoats. None of the subjects were smiling.

Karen returned, her heels tapping against the shiny marbled floor. She handed Luke a flute of Chablis.

"What do you think?" she asked looking around the room.

"I think you've moved up in the world, Karen," he said with a smile.

"All set." April walked in. She had sent the babysitter home and changed her clothes, now wearing a long velvet robe revealing her ample, tanned cleavage, and the ponytail undone, her long hair draping her shoulders. "Why don't we go downstairs and listen to some music?"

The downstairs was an equally ample space with a large-screen TV and an elaborate sound system, the floor covered with plush oriental rugs. Oddly, in an alcove at the far end of the room, partly hidden by sheer drapery, was a king-sized round bed with mirrored ceiling and a bar against a wall.

"I have to tell you Luke, when Karen told me she knew you, I told her you had the best ass of all the jockeys; you know, when you're on a horse," remarked April, sitting with her legs under her on the plush couch, the sound of soft jazz in the air.

It was the weirdest compliment Luke had ever received from anyone.

But what happened later was even more bizarre.

Luke lay on the bed covered by a satin sheet, his casted leg resting on a pillow. With great care and mindful of his still-not-fully healed injuries, the three engaged in what Luke would always remember as an experience like no other.

"I'll be right back sweetie. We're out of wine; I'll get another bottle upstairs." A fully nude April said leaving the bed. Karen, also totally exposed, rested her chin on her right hand, the other under the cover teasing Luke.

With April away from the room, Luke finally spoke, "Karen, who the hell is this woman?"

"I told you, she's my boss."

"How long has she been training horses?" Having been on the racetrack for the past several years, Luke had never seen or heard of her before.

"Oh, she's only been training since last summer." Karen said, "She's Donnie's ex-wife."

"Donnie who?'

"Well, his name is really Donato Giordano, but everybody calls him Donnie."

Luke sat up in a rush, "Donnie Giordano? The pictures upstairs! You mean the mobster?"

Before she could answer, he rebuked: "Karen, how in the fuck do you get me involved in something like this? Are you fucking nuts?"
Half-dressed, he made his way up the stairs, his wooden crutches dragging behind him. He slipped on his one shoe and bolted out the door.

Indicted for the murders of two government informers in 1964, the Donnie Giordano case had been the stuff of front-page news for the previous two years, until finally acquitted of the charges several months before.

For Luciano "Luke" Nodarse, it was the longest ride home of his life.

PART FOUR

Having received the green light from his doctors in the middle of August, by this time racing had switched to Rockingham Park, Luke started getting on horses. A week later, he felt ready to resume riding races. When entries were drawn that day, determined to start Luke back easy, Paul Dwyer scheduled him on only three horses—two of which won.

The next day, the headlines of the sports pages of the area's press heralded "The kid is back!" He was again the toast of the town. Every wise guy in southern New England boasted knowing Luke personally. The ones who were able to get to him requested his appearance at one of the several late-night private clubs for a drink. But it was not to be, for Dwyer scripted every move his hot commodity made. To make sure, the agent had his own guys keeping eyes on the young jockey after business hours.

On the first day of racing back in April of that year, the Suffolk Downs board of stewards visited the jockeys' quarters to welcome the riders and to go over a list of do's and don'ts. It was made clear by the chief steward to, "Stay away from the beach."

In those days, just a stone's throw from the racetrack, Revere Beach featured amusement rides and a variety of games of chance. It was also the site of several popular honky-tonks, some of which were known to be owned or operated by the Mob.

Luke rented a small apartment at the far end of the beach. Four doors away from his building was a small tavern that catered to a quieter clientele than other bars at the opposite end of the beach. Aside from cocktails, the *Sans Souci* also served light meals, as the soft music from a jukebox entertained the usually older customers. It was there one night Luke caught sight of Tom Sweeny sitting with Sam Bruno, the veteran rider who had caused the spill when Luke was hurt. With them at a table in a dark corner were two men Luke did not know, but who needed no neon signs to be recognized as wise guys.

Not wanting to be seen by them, Luke left and went to a restaurant he frequented not far away from the beach. Finishing a small steak, baked potato and a beer, he was glad not to be approached by anyone wanting to talk about horses. He went back to his apartment and turned on the TV.

Two hours later, with the TV still on, Luke was in bed almost asleep when the front door buzzer sounded. He got up and pressed the switch to the speaker, "Yes?"

"Luke it's me, Tom. Are you awake?"

"I am now. What do you want?" asked Luke.

"Hey, I need to speak to you for a couple of minutes. It can't wait until tomorrow."

Luke took his finger off the switch and sighed. "What could he possibly want." He pressed the buzzer to open the front door.
Seconds later, Tom was at the door of the apartment. "Man, I'm glad I got to you tonight."

"I'm glad you're glad," mumbled Luke. "What is it?"
Look, there's something going down in a race you're riding tomorrow."

Now at attention, and with a furrowed brow, Luke asked, "What do you mean something going on?"

"Luke, I know these guys that want to make a play for the trifecta tomorrow in the seventh race. They know we're friends, and wanted me to offer you some cash, two grand, to finish no better than fourth. You're on the morning line favorite in the race."

"Tom, you've got some fucking nerve coming to me with one of your schemes," Luke said angrily, "Look, get away from me. Tell your 'guys' I'm not interested. Now get out," he shouted pushing Tom toward the door.

"Luke, you don't know who you're messing with. These are bad guys. They won't take no for an answer."

"Out!" Luke shouted again.

With Tom gone, Luke sat down thinking. He knew Tom had been hanging around with a bad crowd. The trainer he was working for was from somewhere in the southwest where he had been ruled off the track for three years for a rash of illegal activities. The man stayed away from racing for 10 years and resurfaced months before in Rhode Island where he was granted a conditional license to train horses. The rumors around the track were that this guy would rather cheat for a buck than earn two legally.

Over the last year, he realized that his friendship with Tom was harmful to Luke's success as a jockey. He had been trying to keep him at arm's length. It had become obvious several weeks earlier when Luke walked into the bathroom of the jockeys' room and saw a hand passing money under the partition to someone in the next stall. Luke walked out and went back to his locker but watched to see who came out of the bathroom. Minutes later, he saw Tom and his new mentor, Sam Bruno.

Ever since it happened, Luke had been suspicious but was now convinced the spill in which he was hurt was definitely intentional.
It was the life Tom Sweeny had always dreamed of. Born to poor parents who spent their lives working in sweat shop factories in western Massachusetts, the racetrack and becoming a jockey had made him the envy of his town's gang of young hoodlums, which he always wanted to join. Instead, his slight build and big ears always made him the butt of their jokes.

But he had gotten even. Although he didn't ride for big outfits like Luke, or win as many races, he got along riding pick up mounts for small stables, winning races here and there.

In short order, he got involved with veterans like Sam Bruno, and his band of shady characters. Bruno was at the sunset of his profession and never rode much, his career amounted to that of the outlaw who eked out a living with scams that saw him cashing a bet now and then. To him, Tom was another way to the cashier windows and a return to Boston's flashy club culture where he could connive new suckers looking for that big score. By becoming Bruno's protégé, quickly, Tom saw holding horses and cheating for a price as the best way to keep himself in expensive clothes, a glitzy sports car and some cash in his pocket.

Soon, the underworld took notice.

14

The Fenway, aptly named for the nearby venerable stadium home of the Boston Red Sox, was by some accounts the best nightclub north of New York City. The venue showcased local bands, and regularly featured nationally known rock and roll groups of that era, often without a cover charge. On weekends, the music and the consumption of alcohol and drugs drew throngs of young people from the nearby colleges and universities to keep the place open into the wee hours of the next morning.

It wasn't a secret that the Irish Mob had a hand in the club. The manager, the proverbial tall, dark and handsome Jimmy D'Angelo seemed out of place, as he was Italian. Nevertheless, he was the man every girl wanted to be with and all guys wanted to emulate. He was also an associate of the city's other crime family known as the Irish Mob, and the chief peddler of drugs at the club.

It was generally accepted that the north end of Boston was the turf of the Giordano crime family. The Irish controlled Southie, the south side of the city. Clashes between the two groups were rare, as both respected their boundaries. It was also known that the Giordano Mob was the more politically influential while the Southie group was more ruthless.

"Hello Jimmy; meet my friend Tom Sweeny," said Sam Bruno one late night at The Fenway.

"Oh, you're the jockey. Glad to know you, Tom," said D'Angelo as they shook hands. "What can I get you to drink?" asked D'Angelo. "I know Sam will have his usual draft."

He served the drinks and asked if they had come alone. "What's the matter Tom, no girlfriend?"

"I'm afraid not. I don't have one," Tom said.

"I can fix that; wait here a minute," D'Angelo said as he cleared the counter with a swift leap.

"Hey Jimmy, is Big Al here?" asked Bruno.

"Yeah, he's in the back handicapping Monday's races. I'll be right back, Tom."

As promised, D'Angelo came back followed by a pretty coed who obviously had too much to drink. "Stacy, say hello to my friend Tom. You like horses, right? He's a jockey."

Tom chatted with the girl for a few minutes. She said she was there with three of her girlfriends from school, and proceeded to write the phone number of her dorm on a napkin. "Call me sometime." she said as she returned to her group.

Noticing the girl walking away, Jimmy asked, "Hey what happened, Tom? Where's she going?"

"She gave me her phone number, but went back to the girls she's with."

"Hang on, man. I'll get you one you can take home with you tonight."

For Tom, there would be a price to pay for D'Angelo's generosity that night

15

After its inaugural in 1935, Suffolk Downs quickly became the grandest racing venue in New England, as large and enthusiastic crowds filled the stands every racing day. From the beginning, its marquee event, the Massachusetts Handicap, quickly established its prominence in the American racing calendar by yearly attracting the best and most famous horses and jockeys in the country. Surviving several changes of ownership during the ensuing years, the trend continued for the next four decades, always maintaining the quality racing New England had come to expect.

But the glory days took a turn in the late 1970s, as racing at Suffolk Downs began to dwindle, thus, reducing the racetrack's importance. The area mostly became an outlet for racing stock no longer competitive at major venues around the country.

On the plus side, however, the modest quality of the competition gave many local horsemen a measure of success unattainable in other parts. The circuit of two racetracks to the south and one to the north of Boston made possible the convenience of basically year-round racing within driving distance, thus, ending the need for horsemen to move their operations and their families every few weeks.

On the downside, the sustained notion that New England had become a breeding ground for corruption led some in the industry to question the reputation of their counterparts from that area.

It was that cruel connotation of New England's reputation that prompted Luke to consider, halfway through his second year of riding, that a move elsewhere was vital if his success was to flourish.

PART FIVE

"Your business is riding horses," Paul Dwyer told Luke. "So if there's a horse to ride, God damn it, you ride him. You can't win races playing cards in the jocks' room. Don't question why I put you on any horse. My business is to make you win races. If that doesn't suit you, then you need to get someone else to handle your book."

The scolding came about one day when Luke questioned Dwyer's decision to accept a call on a horse rumored to be a rogue tough to ride. Dwyer took exception to Luke's query.

His agent was right. The horse won without consequence, and Luke never again questioned Dwyer's reasoning when it came to mounts.

One particularly wet and muddy day at Rockingham, Luke rode six horses, and the best he could do was to finish third on one of them. After his last mount in the eighth race, Luke's intention was to clean up and take a girl he had been after out to dinner and hoping that the dinner was nice enough for her to spend the night at his apartment.

After getting his foot hurt in the starting gate incident in the eighth race that afternoon, a jockey got permission from the stewards to take off his remaining mount in the ninth race, leaving the clerk of scales the task of finding a replacement rider. More often than not, there was always a jockey hanging around hoping to pick up a mount. On this dreary day, however, there was no one.

Luke's locker was a few feet away from the clerk of scales' desk, and he heard the official mumble that the stewards were going to have to scratch the horse since there wasn't a replacement jockey. The clerk was about to call the stewards when Luke remembered Dwyer's words spoken in anger: "If there's a horse to ride, you ride him!"

"I'll ride him, Ed," Luke told the clerk, who thanked him and quickly called the stewards and the track announcer with the change of rider. In his haste to put on his riding togs again, Luke didn't have time to look at the program and Racing Form he kept in his locker to see who the trainer of the horse was, the odds in the program and the past performances of the horse, something he did as a rule to have an idea of how the race would develop.

Actually, the horse was 20-1 in the program, and the odds would have been much higher by post time had Luke not been the rider. The eight-year-old gelding had been off the board in his previous seven starts, had not raced in three months and had made little money in purses in its lifetime. The trainer had four or five horses in a lean-to barn at the far end of the backside, as the stable area was commonly called, where no other trainer wanted to be. His help consisted of his wife and three kids. In every sense of the word, this trainer was a gyp, the racetrack's parlance for gypsy, or a low-end operation.

In the paddock, Luke shook hands with the trainer, who thanked him profusely for accepting the mount. Never would one of the leading riders consider riding one of this trainer's horses under normal circumstances. The trainer introduced Luke to the owner and his wife.

"Luke, these are the owners, Bob Napolitano and Mrs. Napolitano." Luke shook hands with the man and tipped his cap at the wife. At first glance, Napolitano's face seemed familiar to Luke. In the post parade on the way to the starting gate, Luke racked his brain trying to recall where he had seen the man before but was unable to place him.

It was a time when agent Dwyer's chiding proved right yet again. The pickup mount ran the race of its life to win at odds of 40 to 1. Luke himself could not believe it. Upon his return to the winner's circle the overjoyed trainer and his family, and the ecstatic owners were slapping high fives as they posed for the photo. Once Luke dismounted, the owner's wife gave him a big hug and a kiss on the cheek, and Bob Napolitano placed a win ticket in Luke's hand as he shook it. It was the owners' and the trainer's first win in over a year.

PART SIX

Early in 1910, teenage brothers Silvio and Alphonse Giordano arrived at Ellis Island. They began their journey on a ship carrying hundreds of people from their native Sicily, where their father, Tomassino, worked in a sulfur mine. Three years earlier, a coworker named Antonio Lucania immigrated to America with his family. A few years after their arrival, one of the Lucania boys, a teenager by the name of Salvatore was on his way to becoming perhaps the most feared mobster in the U.S. His friends called him, "Lucky."

Once in New York, the Giordano brothers found their way to the Lower East Side in the borough of Manhattan, at that time, a popular destination for Italian immigrants. As instructed by their father the two teenagers sought out the Lucania family, who gladly gave the youngsters shelter until they found jobs and got to know the city. Quickly, they became comfortable in their new surroundings, enjoying a life far different from the one they had left behind in Italy. Convinced that jobs were for poor people, the brothers quickly became attracted by the life of crime led by Lucky, who was on his way to the top of New York's underworld.

Initiated in the gang years later, and with Lucky's backing, the Giordano brothers started their own operation in Massachusetts. By instilling intimidation and fear in Boston's large Italian immigrant population, they found success dealing with corruption of every kind: bootlegging; interstate transportation and distribution of illegal tobacco products; narcotics, including gambling and prostitution. Eventually, they infiltrated and controlled worker's unions, not to mention their connection with the urban machine of politicians that, for self-gain, bolstered the Giordano Mob's influence in their precincts. Indeed, their boldness quickly earned them the reputation of the most powerful crime family north of New York.

In 1959, while on a business trip to Chicago accompanied by his two bodyguards, older brother Silvio Giordano suffered a fatal heart attack in his compartment on a passenger train. His burial in Boston was attended by representatives of Mob families as far away as Kansas City, along with multiple bouquets of flowers from Las Vegas and Los Angeles.

The surviving younger brother, Alphonse, carried on the successful operation. Four years after taking over, he was diagnosed with terminal liver cancer at 72 years of age.

A year before his death, and suffering from his disease, the sickly uncle handpicked his nephew Donato to take control of the family's business. Two conditions for the appointment were to end his marriage to "that Irish whore" from the south side and get out of the race horse business. Those were the last orders he would make as head of the Giordano family; two days later, he died in his sleep.

Both conditions were quickly met. After the burial of his uncle three days later, Donnie resolved the issue by coldly and unceremoniously telling his wife April their quickie Vegas marriage was over, and as parting gifts she could keep the stable of horses as well as their sprawling suburban home.

As if this were not enough, and still reeling from Donnie's directive, April asked, "What about the baby?"

They had recently learned April was pregnant, "The kid will always be a Giordano and never will go without," Donnie said. "Don't you worry about that."

Days later in his ample office on the top floor of Angie's Inn and Supper Club overlooking Massachusetts's Bay, Donnie held his first meeting as head of the family with three of his henchmen. At the conclusion of the day's agenda, disregarding his uncle's parting condition, Donnie commented as an afterthought, "By the way, as far as the horserace back in June, while the plus 100 large was a nice score, it would be better if we could get that Cuban kid to play along. I mean, we can't go dropping a jockey in a race every time we want to make a score." After a brief pause, Donnie continued, "I know you guys have tried to bring him into the fold without results, but you need to get it done."

From an early age, Donnie Giordano knew his family wielded power. After two years at Dartmouth, he quit school and went back to Boston to join the family business. Although at first there was resentment from other relatives who believed that at the age of 42 he was too young to be named capo, Donnie quickly gained the admiration of his elders for his prowess as a cunning negotiator. On the same week of his appointment, he orchestrated the brutal killing of two would-be informers trying to infiltrate the family in return for leniency from the cops for their own petty crimes.

About buying off the young jockey, "I still can't believe he turned down Sweeny," retorted Nick Rosetti on a sofa chair facing Donnie. "Shit, I know guys that would kill a priest for two grand."

Nicola Rosetti was Donnie's closest confidant within the inner circle. He was the son of upper-middle-class emigrants. Upon arrival in Boston as a young man fresh out of medical school, his father quickly became the go to MD for the large Italian communities of the North End and East Boston. His mother, a school teacher in the old country, was tapped as principal of a local high school, mostly due to her husband's association with the underworld and the fact that she spoke English. A year behind Donnie, Nick also graduated from the elite boys' school in Andover, where they became best friends. But the many rules and regulations of such an institution ran counter to two carefree Italian boys prone to mischief who never felt comfortable among their non-Italian blue-blooded classmates.

"Yeah, Nick, but you have to understand that $2000 doesn't mean anything to this kid. Hell, you see all the races he's winning. He makes many times that much just by riding winners," said Bob Napolitano sitting on the armchair next to Nick. "Let me figure out another way to go about it," he said.

Napolitano was a different story. Coming from a family of peasant immigrants and of little consequence, he was accepted only because of his ethnic name and his willingness to be the family's errand boy. From his early association with the family, old man Al Giordano kept him busy looking over low-end rackets, the numbers game and shylocks in the city but barred him from the larger illegal activities. Nevertheless, Napolitano enjoyed his imagined influence as a connected guy, which afforded him a decent living enabling him to indulge his wife's taste for garish extravagance.

It was a mere coincidence that Luke Nodarse won a race on Napolitano's one and only racehorse when the originally scheduled jockey took off the mount due to an injury the race before. Informed that Donnie wanted to have the young jockey under the family's control, he immediately said he'd get the job done as a way of gaining favor with the new capo.

Seated silently with his head leaning back against the leather couch was Johnny "Babe" Bonaventura, for years in charge of the band of soldiers that were the family's muscle. His motto, "Shoot first and don't bother asking questions," was the same it had been when he did his first job at age 13, killing a storekeeper for a gold watch and $20. Now at 66, he'd do it for nothing.

The morning following the win on the horse owned by Bob Napolitano, as is the custom of many riders, Luke went to the barn to again thank the trainer for the winning mount.

"Are you kidding? Thank you," said the trainer, as a new Lincoln Continental drove up to the barn.

Bob Napolitano stepped out of the car wearing a silk suit that was probably made to order but tacky nevertheless. The shirt unbuttoned halfway exposing his hairy chest, a big plastic red pepper hanging from a gold chain around his neck. He tip-toed in his two-tone shoes careful not to step in the puddles made by the running water hose. With a big smile on his face, he shook Luke's hand and said, "Madonna! What a great ride," and like his wife the day before, gave the rider a big hug.

It was meant to be only a quick courtesy visit for Luke to go to the barn, but Napolitano couldn't stop talking.

"You know Luke, I'd like to take you to dinner. There's a new Italian restaurant nearby in Lawrence. It's a family joint. I did the owner a little favor years ago. How about it?"

"Mr. Napolitano, that's not necessary," Luke said, "I thank you for the mount very much, but you'll have to excuse me. I have horses to work on the other side."

"Oh, that's all right, Luke. I understand. We'll talk more when I pick you up in the jocks' room tomorrow after you get done. We'll go eat."

Still, Luke couldn't place where he'd seen the man before.

The next afternoon, Luke exited the jockeys' room after his last ride. As he opened the chain link gate leading to the parking lot, he was glad Napolitano wasn't there.

He walked toward his car. As he neared his Buick, he saw the white Lincoln parked next to it, and Napolitano shouting from his opened window, "Come on Luke, this pasta is gonna be the best you ever had."

There was no getting away from Bob Napolitano.

Upon entering the little restaurant, the owner, wearing a white tee shirt and a long and stained white apron tied under his large belly, did everything but kiss Napolitano's ring as he took his order. A young waiter rushed toward the table with a bottle of wine in hand, and quickly opened the Chianti Riserva, offering the cork to Napolitano, who brusquely waved him away.

Luke had to admit the dinner was great. As Napolitano ordered, the pasta was al dente, the veal scaloppini so tender it could be cut with a fork. The basket of warm bread was filled three times. To round off, Napolitano ordered Tiramisu "only if it's fresh!" and café espresso with a shot of Sambuca, which Luke didn't care for. The man ate like he was going to the guillotine.

As if to spoil the sumptuous feast, however, horses and racing were the only sources of conversation. Nearly two hours later, Napolitano asked for the bill, and with his hand on his chest and bowing his head, the owner spoke to him in Italian. Since no money was exchanged, Luke supposed the dinner was on the house.

Driving him back to his car, Napolitano asked Luke if he was going to the horsemen's awards banquet the following Saturday night. Usually, Luke avoided those gatherings, the rule of thumb being that certain horsemen had the tendency of drinking too much and saying things they later regretted.

"No, I don't think so," he said. "I heard it's a sellout anyway." Luke knew he'd made a mistake as soon as he said it.

"Luke, I bought a table of eight. I'd like you to come as my guest."
"God, no!" Luke thought to himself.

"You got a girl? Susi and I'd like to meet her. If you don't, no problem. Susi's younger sister is a real knockout. We'll fix yous up." But as if that wasn't enough: "I'll give you directions to my house in Wakefield. We'll go from there."

"How about if you give me your phone number, and I'll let you know," said Luke.

"You know what, better than that, I'll call you in the jockeys' room Wednesday. But don't let me down. We'll have a good time."

Even though Luke had had enough of Bob Napolitano to last a lifetime, he couldn't get away from the man. When he called Wednesday, Luke asked if there were two extra seats at the table, he'd like to invite his valet Cosmo and his wife to come along. Luke needed a buffer and Cosmo loved to talk.

"Sure, sure," Napolitano said. "Bring him along; tell him to meet us at the joint."

Saturday evening Luke drove to Napolitano's house. It was a big double-decker in a nice neighborhood midway between Salem, New Hampshire and Boston; it didn't look very old. Aside from the Lincoln, there was a red Thunderbird in the driveway and a white Cadillac in the two-car garage.

Napolitano welcomed him at the door wearing a dark burgundy tuxedo. Luke found the furniture and everything else in the house flashy and garish, matching Napolitano's suit. He offered Luke a glass of wine, "I buy it by the case; they ship it to me from the old country," he boasted. "The women are upstairs getting ready. Wait 'til you see my sister-in-law, Madonna. You'll want to take her home with you," he said as he kissed the fingertips of his cupped right hand.

Luke asked if he could use the bathroom. "Sure, sure. It's at the top of the stairs, first door on the left."

As he entered and closed the door, the gaudy décor made him shake his head. There was also one other distinctive feature, a wall telephone next to the toilet. Who the hell is this guy that needs a phone in the bathroom?

Upon returning downstairs, Luke told Napolitano he had never seen a telephone in a bathroom.

"In my line of business, I always have to be available." He left it at that.

The sister-in-law was indeed very pretty and petite, with beautiful olive-colored skin. She wore a light-blue chiffon dress that accentuated her lovely figure. She spoke very softly. *In all, not bad for a blind date*, Luke thought. But it wasn't long before he realized that she wasn't impressed to be accompanied by someone less than six feet tall. That he was a successful jockey didn't mean as much to her as it did to her brother-in-law. When Luke told Cosmo about the banquet, he said, "Cos, the guy is all yours. Do your part and chew his ear off." Thank heaven he did.

It was a full house. The award ceremony took up over an hour before dinner was served. When the emcee, a member of the turf press corps trying his best to be funny, announced the recipient of the silver plate for leading owner, an older man native of Poland stood up as the gathering applauded. As he neared the dais, he brought down the house when his wife called his attention to his open fly. He said some words in his native language as he pulled up the zipper before receiving his trophy. His long-winded acceptance speech was barely understood due to his thick accent. Nevertheless, the audience gave him a loud round of applause.

The band played and the dance floor was put to good use. Luke's date declined the invitation to dance, so he excused himself and milled around greeting some of his clients. While speaking to an owner and his wife, he felt someone tap his shoulder. He turned to see the ex-Mrs. Giordano in a black dress that must have been painted on her.

"Hello Luke," she said gently putting her arm under his, and telling the owner and his wife, "Please excuse us. I need to speak to Luke about a horse he's going to ride for me this week."

As she led him away, Luke spoke first, "Look April, we have nothing to talk about. What happened was a mistake."

"Oh, Luke," she said. "You have nothing to worry about. I'm a divorced woman, and I like to have a good time. And I like you. My ex understands."

"It's been nice seeing you again April. Please excuse me." He walked back to the safe territory of his uninterested date, sat down and had another sip of wine.

Mrs. Napolitano talked all the way home. Her husband was uncharacteristically quiet; he seemed worried about something. Earlier, as dinner was being served, Napolitano stepped outside of the hall to speak to two men who were not guests at the banquet. When he came back, his festive mood was gone.

Luke thanked Mr. and Mrs. Napolitano and the sister-in-law. He made a tongue-in-cheek remark that he had a great time. The young rider made it a point to tell Paul Dwyer to avoid riding for this owner again.

18

"What are you guys doing here?" asked Napolitano as he walked toward the two men standing in the shadows outside the venue.
"The question is what are you doing here? Donnie wants to know what's happening," said the older of the two. He was rotund and small in stature; the dark trench coat and fedora made him almost invisible in the darkness.

The other man was taller and much younger. His sinister countenance and the steely look of a thug were unmistakable.

"Hey Babe, I said it was going to take time; the kid's not there yet," said the nervous Napolitano.

With a finger to Napolitano's face the smaller man threatened, "Donnie said if you can't do it, he'll send someone that can."

With the intimidation delivered, both men turned and walked away. Johnny "Babe" Bonaventura's last words were, "Bobby, you're hanging by a thread here."

His night spoiled, Napolitano went back to his table.

19

Several weeks after the horsemen's banquet, Vince Muller hired a new hot walker. He was a tall man in his early-forties, who looked nothing like the people who usually worked on the backside of a racetrack. He dressed in pressed khakis, laundered madras shirts and leather loafers. He wore his hair short and neat and had nothing much to say other than hello. Luke knew him by the name of Benjamin.

"We have nothing for you this morning, Luke," Vince said to the young rider one morning. "It's an easy day; Marcelo can get on the two trackers."

"Thanks, Vince. I'll see you in the paddock this afternoon," said Luke as he turned to leave.

"Oh, I almost forgot," said Vince, "Benjamin the hot walker is looking for you. He went to the track kitchen to find you."

"I'll look for him," he said. *What does he want with me?* Luke wondered.

As he neared the track's kitchen, Luke saw the hot walker coming out of the swinging doors. "Hey, Benjamin, you want to see me?"

"Yes, Luke. I need to talk to you. Let's walk over to my car," he said.

Luke was puzzled. They walked past the line of parked cars along the fence in front of the track kitchen until they reached a fairly new, dark blue Ford Mustang.

"Here, get in," Benjamin said as he unlocked his door and pressed the button to open the passenger's side.

The mystery grew when Benjamin reached for his wallet in his rear pocket. "Luke, I'm with the FBI," he said showing Luke his I.D. "My name is Louis Hamm. Here's my business card. Keep it."

Luke took the card, "What's this about? What do you want with me?" he asked with a creased brow.

"I need to show you some pictures," said the agent reaching for a manila envelope under his bucket seat. With the envelope in hand, he said, "I don't think you're in any trouble right now. I just have a few questions, but you need to know that anything you say can be used against you if we end up in court. If you think you need an attorney before talking to me, you both can come to my office in Boston, and I'll ask my questions there."

"Look, Benjamin, or whatever your name is, I haven't done anything wrong, so go ahead and ask your question, and I'll decide if I'm going to answer," a disturbed Luke said.

Hamm opened the envelope, pulling out a series of 8 by 10 black and white prints. Handing Luke the first photograph, he asked, "Do you know this man?"

Luke was more startled than ever, "He's a horse owner. His name is Bob Napolitano. What about him?"

"It's all right, Luke. Let me show these others," Hamm said. "Who are these two guys talking to Napolitano? If you know."

Luke took the picture, and looking at it, he replied, "You know that I know who they are. They are riders, Tom Sweeny and Sam Bruno." Luke paused. It immediately came to him where he had seen Napolitano before. He was one of the two men seating with Tom and Bruno at the *Sans Souci* one night. But Luke revealed nothing.

"Now Luke, you said Napolitano is a horse owner. Is he also a friend of yours?" The agent handed Luke another picture of Luke and Napolitano with two women entering the horsemen's banquet hall weeks before.

"He's not really my friend. By chance, I rode a winner for him and he invited me to the banquet. I didn't even want to go," Luke explained.

"But you have been in his company more than once." He passed a picture of the two of them coming out of the Italian restaurant in Lawrence.

"Look, I don't care what you think. The guy is a pest. I didn't want to go there with him either."

"Does he talk about horses or racing? Has he ever asked you to do anything?"

"This is the last thing I'm going to say to you, and I'm getting out of the car." Luke was visibly upset. "Yes, all he talks about is horses. That's why I don't like being around him. But he has never asked me to do anything," he said, opening the door of the car, "If you want to talk to me anymore, I think I will have that attorney present." He got out and slammed shut the car door.

20

Away from their unlawful enterprise, horse racing was the pastime of choice for many members of Boston's Giordano Mob. From the time he was a young man, Donnie Giordano enjoyed the ponies. Yearly, he rented a private box in the coveted area near the finish line during the season at Suffolk Downs. He could be found there after the second race most racing afternoons in the company of two or three of his henchmen, testing their handicapping prowess with a racing form, and backing their choices at the same $100-dollar window. Unable to keep a low profile in their silk attire and high heeled shoes, everybody in the clubhouse was aware of them as they called attention to themselves loudly urging their picks as the horses neared the finish of each race.

On an afternoon when he lost over a thousand dollars, Donnie drove back to the club with his main lieutenant, Nick Rosetti. "Fuhgetaboutit. The best way to win at the track is to have the damned race fixed," Donnie said glibly.

"Hey, I'm in for that," Rosetti replied. "Hell, I'm sure trainers and jockeys take those kinds of shots all the time."

"We need to talk with that boob, Napolitano. He's got to get this thing done. He owns a couple of nags and knows all the players. We could use his trainer and his jockey."

Several days later, while watching the post parade from his clubhouse box, Donnie noticed a young woman sitting in the adjacent box along with three older people who owned a horse racing later in the afternoon. Her black hair loosely hanging over her low-cut, white dress, brazenly exposing her tanned cleavage. She was lost in thought reading her racing program when Donnie moved closer to her and whispered in her ear with a grin, "Does money make you passionate?"
Smiling, she turned to him and answered, "That's the most provocative come-on I've ever heard. I don't know what to say." He told her his name was Donnie. She introduced herself as April Donahue.

After cocktails at Angie's Inn and Supper Club in Swampscott at the conclusion of the day's racing, they drove Route 1A, past Suffolk Downs toward the Sumner tunnel. As they exited, the car turned right entering the north end. Stella's was the landmark restaurant favored by the city's upper crust Italians, where the cuisine far exceeded its location at the end of a dark and out-of-the-way alley in the city's Little Italy. Warmly greeted by long-time maître di' Alberto, they were led to Donnie's usual booth in a secluded corner of the dining room. The two bodyguards took a table at the bar by the front entrance.

After the usual first date flirtation and playful teasing that often leads two people to a predestined amorous encounter, their conversation got around to racing. Finding out that Donnie had once thought of owning a horse, April said she always dreamed of being a racehorse trainer. They agreed to talk about a possible partnership. After the luscious meal, they passed up the dessert tray opting instead to return to Donnie's private suite at Angie's.

Donnie Giordano and April Donahue became inseparable. Doing business as Bay State Stables, they attended horse sales in Kentucky and Florida, assisted by a young veterinarian introduced to them by Bob Napolitano, who also went along. However, they found that the prices at those venues were more than they wanted to spend on horses that would primarily race in New England. Not to go away empty handed, however, they encountered a local trainer from whom they purchased two geldings, a four- and a six-years-old, that had been racing in claiming races at Latonia, a minor racetrack in northern Kentucky.

Flying high at their prospects, the next morning they boarded a United Airlines flight from Louisville to Las Vegas, and after two days and two nights of too much booze and little sleep, Donnie and April were married at a 24-hour drive-through chapel just off the strip. Napolitano stood as best man.
In three months' time, the new couple put together a 12-horse stable with Napolitano's trainer looking after the string long enough for April to get her trainer's license. It wouldn't take long. Giordano saw to it by entrusting Napolitano to take care of it.

21

The one-hour drive from Suffolk Downs to suburban Foxboro, where the Suffolk Downs' association steward lived, was always prolonged by the heavy southbound rush hour traffic. Napolitano found out that the steward would usually stop for a drink to wait for the traffic to dissipate.

By coincidence, the stewards' preferred watering hole was the bar at the nearby Angie's Inn and Supper Club, which unbeknownst to him was owned by the Giordano family.

One afternoon after the races, the association steward was "accidently" engaged by Bob Napolitano sitting two stools away. "That was some stretch run the nine horse made to nose out the favorite in the last race," Napolitano directed the comment at the official.

"His best races are usually charging from way back," commented the steward, taking the bait.

For the next several days Napolitano made his way to Angie's, by now sitting next to the steward sharing drinks and chatting about the day's races.

One afternoon, it was a slow time at Angie's when Napolitano and the steward were the only two customers. A shapely red-headed young woman came in and caught the eye of the steward as she walked to the other side of the oval-shaped counter. When the bartender approached her, they started chatting as if they knew each other.

"That is certainly a good-looking head," said the association steward, nodding toward the woman.

"You like her, Larry?" By now the two men were on a first name basis. "I can do you some good there."

Surprised, the steward responded with a giggle, "No, Bob. It's all right."

"No, no. I mean it." Napolitano got up, walked to the end of the counter and called the bartender over. In a whisper, he asked, "Is that the girl, Tommy?"

"Yeah. Her name is Samantha. She works out of here sometimes."

With this information, Napolitano walked around the bar and approached the attractive Samantha.

"Hi. My name is Bob, and I know who you are."

Somewhat startled by the approach, Samantha said hello.

"Let me ask you, Samantha, what would it cost me to fix you up with my friend over there?" said Napolitano nodding toward the steward.

The woman hesitated for a minute before answering, "Fifty dollars for a half hour."

"Wow, for that price you must be really good," said Napolitano smiling as he reached for the roll of cash in his pocket. "Here you go dear. Go to the front desk and tell the girl you need the keys to Bob's room. I'll give you five or ten minutes to get ready, and I'll send him over. Make sure you show him a good time now," he said with a smile.

The woman left the bar and Napolitano returned to his stool next to his new friend Larry.

"You're all set Larry. Her name is Samantha. She's waiting for you in room 16. It's a room I keep here to stay in sometimes when my wife is in a bad mood."

"You're kidding me, right? a surprised Larry said, again giggling. "Gees, Bob, you didn't have to do that."

"Go ahead Larry. It'll make your ride home that much smoother."

Napolitano waited ten minutes after Larry went to meet his date, threw $50 on the counter and said see you later to the bartender.

"Hi, Mary. May I have a key to my room, please."

"Hi, Bob. I gave one to a girl that asked for it a little while ago," said the hotel clerk.

"Yeah, I told her to wait for me there."

Walking down the hallway, Napolitano approached room 16. Silently, he unlocked the door and peeked in.

In the king-sized bed, a nude Larry with his black socks still on was above the woman moaning in ecstasy. Napolitano reached for the small Instamatic in his coat pocket and snapped the picture. He then closed the door and without making any noise, returned to the lobby to wait for a satisfied and smiling Larry.

After one more encounter at Angie's the following afternoon, an understanding was agreed upon by Napolitano and the steward leading to the issuance of a horse trainer's license to April. The customary testing expected from a candidate for such a license was not required for this special case.

Stung by the experience, the 57-year old racing official realized he was better off stalled in crawling traffic listening to talk radio, rather than at a bar having a drink with a stranger who turned out to be a swindler. His job and marriage were worth preserving, no matter the hair color of a temporary distraction.

22

At the conclusion of Rockingham that year, David Raymond finished as the leading trainer in New Hampshire, and while Luke was not the leading rider, he did well enough to finish third behind two veterans in the standings but bested all the other five apprentices at the meet.

Winners had come at a fast clip for Luke. The horses he rode for Raymond were mostly favorites or near favorites, and always figured to run well. Other owners and trainers had taken notice of the young rider and were eager to engage him to ride their horses. For a tyro, he was adept at keeping his mounts free of trouble in races, earning him praise from his clients. The swift switching of his whip from right to left hand and visa-verse was rare for a novice rider.

Luke possessed a quiet confidence in his ability, thinking of himself as good as any and better than most jockeys. Yet, even he was amazed at the way some longshot mounts with obviously little chance of winning, ran the best races of their lives when he was the rider. Many finishing in front to reward their backers with large payoffs.

The old saw of the racetrack is that an ordinary rider can win on the best horse in a race. In turn, a good jockey can win on an ordinary horse. Some of Luke's winners left veteran racetrackers wondering if the game was on the up and up. Luke himself often thought that some of his winners were the result of fixed races. Whatever the case, young Luke enjoyed the celebrity that came with his success.

Three weeks later, back at Narragansett and night racing, in the last race one bitterly cold night, Luke rode a horse for the trainer of a small stable. When the horse surprised everyone and finished first, bettors set the grandstand's trashcans on fire in a protest that the race had been rigged.

Security guards escorted Luke back to the jockeys' room. The owner of the horse and his son followed close behind. Once away from the crowd, both father and son thanked Luke by handing him a five-dollar win ticket worth $380.00. The son, who was the manager of a popular Boston nightclub, gave the jockey his card and told him to come by for a drink sometime. "Tom Sweeny is a friend of mine and comes by all the time," he said.

Luke would find out later that Jimmy D'Angelo, the owner's son, had close ties with Boston's infamous Irish Mob.

23

Talking with his agent one morning, Luke told Dwyer that he wanted to buy his mother a house. It would be a birthday surprise. Like Luke, Dwyer had come from meager beginnings to become highly successful in his field. He remembered that at the age of 30 he too had bought the home where his elderly parents now lived.

"I think it's a wonderful idea. You can never go wrong investing in real estate. Maybe there's something around your neighborhood.

Days later, Luke spotted a house with a "for sale" sign several streets from his mother's apartment. With his agent the next day they drove to see the brand new double-decker with a for sale sign by the driveway. Men were still putting finishing touches on the facade. Luke and Dwyer pulled up in front and looked at it for a few minutes.

A lady with a clipboard came out from the side door making notes. She noticed the people in the car studying the house and waved. "How about it, Luke? Let's go take a look."

The woman was the owner-realtor of the property. She showed them around; three bedrooms two baths, a nice kitchen-dining room, and a big living room with a brick fireplace.

"Is the house for you?" the woman asked Dwyer.

"No. It's for him and his family," he answered.

"I'm sorry; then who are you?"

"Oh, I'm his agent."

Puzzled, the woman said, "Well, look, the price I quoted includes my commission. What you two work out is separate," she said, thinking Dwyer was Luke's real estate agent.

Too young to take out a mortgage, Luke spoke to his Aunt Lucy, whose name went on the deed. On her birthday, Luke and Lucy took Annie Nodarse to see her new house.

It was the last year of Luke's contract to trainer Raymond. Now on his own and without the apprentice allowance, Luke thought about moving his tack to Miami but decided to stay and ride at Lincoln that winter and enjoy the new home. Paul Dwyer stayed on as his agent.

Making his rounds one cold morning, Luke passed a girl wearing a pink and gray ski suit carrying to-go hot coffee cups in a small cardboard box. As he walked by he looked back at her and said, "I need a ski suit like yours but in navy blue."

"Why don't you buy one?" she said, grinning.

"I don't know where they sell them." he said with a smile, "Maybe you'll take me where you bought yours, and as a sign of gratitude, I'll take you to lunch. My name is Luke."

"I know who you are," she said. "You ride for my father sometimes. I'm Caroline."

"Who's your dad?" Luke asked.

"Bruce Huddleston."

"Really? He is one of my favorite trainers," he said. "Look, I have one more horse to get on and then I'm done for the morning. What if I meet you in front of the track kitchen, and you can lead the way to that store?"

She shrugged still smiling, "Do you usually invite all the girls you pass on the road to lead the way?"

"Only if they are pretty . . . and know where I can buy a blue ski suit," he said. "How about it? See you after I get on this horse?"

"Okay, but come and get me in my father's barn. I need to tell him where I'm going," Caroline said.

"Deal. See you there in about a half hour." He hurried along into the shedrow of a nearby barn.

They sat down in a booth at a little restaurant on the way to the city. Caroline Huddleston had graduated from high school in the spring. She was taking a year off from school before joining her older sister at Mount Vernon College.

When the waitress came to take their order, she immediately recognized Luke. "Hey Mary," she said to the other waitress, "Here is the jockey you bet on the other day when you won the $37 dollars." Mary, the waitress, came over and said she would take their order and deduct a discount from the bill.

Luke cringed at being recognized. As people at other tables turned to look at the jockey, Caroline sat smiling. By the time their order was served, the distraction of fame was over, "Don't you know fame is fleeting?" she teased. Enjoying their breakfast, Caroline answered Luke's question, "I don't really know what to study, maybe law or medicine. I haven't decided yet.

"The three things I need most, a good lawyer, a caring doctor, and a pretty girlfriend," said Luke.

"Gee, you're not the shy type, are you?" Luke would see much of Caroline from then on.

24

Three weeks after speaking to the FBI agent, Luke got in his car in the jocks' parking lot after riding. On the floor of the passenger side, much to his surprise, he saw a crumpled paper bag. Inside, covered neatly in plastic wrapping, were two stacks of hundred dollar bills, each bound together with a thick rubber band. An astonished and confused Luke read the label on each stack "$5000.00." He shook his head and whispered, "Ten thousand dollars." Adding to his bewilderment, inside the bag was a handwritten note with a phone number: "Call me, Bob Napolitano." The jockey was shocked.

Luke had planned to drive to his mother's and stay over, as the next day was a Sunday and no racing. Instead, he drove back to his apartment, where he spent the night looking at the contents of the paper bag and wondering what it was all about. Eventually, he fell asleep on the couch.

When he woke up, still dressed in the clothes he wore the day before, he reached for the phone and dialed the number on the note. After several rings, a man's voice he didn't recognize answered. "Hello. Is Bob there?" Luke asked. "Who's this?" said the man with a brusque tone. Luke quickly hung up, still looking at the two stacks of money. Not knowing what to do, he called his agent. "Paul, I need to see you."

It took Luke one hour to get to the agent's two-story home in Malden, and another thirty minutes to tell him what had happened. Paul Dwyer silently listened to Luke. "Where's the money now?" he asked. "Do you still have the FBI guy's card?" Taking the card from Luke, he said, "Let me call him."

An answering service took the call. Paul left his name and number, and a message that it was important for him to speak to the agent.

Two hours later, Dwyer answered the phone. "Mr. Hamm calling for Mr. Dwyer," said the woman's voice.

"This is Mr. Dwyer." There was a momentary silence as the woman transferred the call.

"Mr. Dwyer, this is Agent Hamm returning your call. What can I do for you?"

Dwyer introduced himself and proceeded to tell the agent about the bundle of money left in Luke's car and the attached note. "Would it be possible for you and Luke to come downtown, and bring the bag? the agent asked, "I'd need to have another agent involved in the Napolitano matter sit in."

Dwyer and Luke rode the elevator to the fifth floor of the government center building the following morning where they promptly met Agent Hamm in the lobby of the FBI office.

Coffee and doughnuts were offered before Hamm and his associate, an agent named Perry, sat across from Dwyer and Luke, and recorded Luke's account of what had transpired in a device on the table.

With the recorder now shut off, the two agents excused themselves to an adjacent room to discuss what steps to take.

Upon their return, Hamm said, "Luke, we need you to call Napolitano from here. Tell him you have the bag he left in your car and want to talk to him about it." He continued, "Don't be nervous. Talk calmly. Don't let him be concerned. Tell him you can see him tomorrow after the races."

Agent Perry spoke, "We are going to give you a little device with a microphone and show you how to put it on before you go meet with Napolitano after you get done riding. It's very easy."

"We'll be listening from a vehicle nearby," Hamm continued," Get out of the car as soon as he tells you what it is he wants you to do. We'll take it from there. Okay, Luke?"

The agent turned on the recorder again as Luke made the call. Napolitano quickly agreed to see the jockey in the Suffolk Down's parking lot after the races the next day.

An hour after Luke and Dwyer left the government office, Babe Bonaventura answered the office phone at Angie's with Donnie and Nick listening to the speaker. The voice at the other end related what had taken place earlier, and the meeting of the jockey and his agent at the FBI's office.

Talking on the phone was Thomas Morrison, a corrupt FBI agent on the Giordano family's payroll.

"Any word on Napolitano?" asked Nick Rosetti as he approached the men sitting at the counter at Angie's.

"It's been four days since we've heard from him," answered "Babe Bonaventura," sitting with two thugs drinking expresso. "I answered a call for him yesterday. They hung up as I said hello. Maybe me and a couple of the boys should go to his house and find out what the hell is going on."

"Yeah, you need to go over there, but before you do, I need to talk to you in the office," said Nick as he started up the stairs.

"Close the door, Babe," said Nick, "I talked to Donnie last night. Have you noticed Napolitano acting strange lately?"

"Yeah, I've noticed," Bonaventura answered. "No telling with that sonofabitch. I know Donnie likes him, but I've never trusted the guy."

"He's been wining and dining that kid Nodarse," said Nick, "But I don't think he's any closer to bringing him around."

"Let me put the fear of God in that kid," retorted Bonaventura, "I'll bring him around."

"Never mind that for now. Just go find Napolitano."

Upon arrival at Napolitano's house an hour later, Bonaventura sent the man in the backseat to ring the doorbell.

A woman wearing a maid's costume answered. She said Mr. Napolitano was not home, and would he like to leave a message.

"Yes. Tell him Donnie wants to see him."

As they drove off, Bonaventura noticed a Ford sedan parked across the street, two houses away from Napolitano's. *Hmm, those guys look like cops*, Bonaventura thought to himself.

Sunday afternoon, Bob Napolitano entered Angie's, "Hello, guys," he said to the men sitting at the counter playing cards.

Upon seeing Napolitano, Babe Bonaventura asked, "Where the fuck have you been? I went to your house yesterday and left word for you to call Donnie."

"I had to run an errand with my wife. We were in New Hampshire and got home late last night." Napolitano said.

"You better go upstairs, see Donnie," Bonaventura told him.

Napolitano knocked on the door and entered. "Hello, boss."

From behind his desk, Donnie said, "You're finally here. I have some stuff to go over with you, but before anything what about the money from last week's collection?"

Napolitano hesitated. "Look, Donnie, I got in a bind and needed to use it. Is it all right if I turn it in a couple of days? Napolitano neglected to tell his boss that he had left the money in Luke's car the day before.

"What, the kid is gonna give it back to you?" he said with a smirk.

Napolitano was stunned.

Donnie jumped up from behind his desk to confront Napolitano angrily. "Where in the hell do you come off leaving my ten grand in somebody's car," he yelled livid with rage.

"Look, Donnie, you know we've offered that kid short money—"

"Never mind that," Donnie cut him off. He turned and reached across the desk to the intercom to the bar, "Send Babe up," he ordered.

Bonaventura came in without knocking.

"Tell Bob what you saw yesterday," Donnie shouted.

Sitting in his regular spot on the leather couch, Bonaventura said to Napolitano, "Do you know that you're being followed?" and proceeded to tell him about the two cops outside his home. "They've probably tailed you here now."

"Why the hell would they be following me?" Napolitano said.

Enraged by the question, Donnie yelled again, "What do you think, coppers don't pay attention? They know you've been trying to bribe that jockey for Christ's sake."

Bonaventura cut in, "This business about an errand in New Hampshire with your wife is bullshit." He accused, "I bet my life you were inside the house hiding when we went by there yesterday."

"How long have the cops been tailing you?" Donnie asked. "Why haven't you said anything instead of walking around here sulking like a moron?" said Donnie pacing the room.

Napolitano's head dropped, as Donnie now stood in front of him, furious with rage.

"I'm sorry boss. I was in Waltham collecting last week when I thought I saw a car following me three or four cars back on the Mass Pike," Napolitano confessed still with his head down, "I got off at the Belmont exit, and it was still behind me. But I was able to lose it in traffic downtown. I didn't see it again until yesterday when I was backing out of my driveway. It was parked across the street, a couple of houses away."

Angrily, Donnie cut him off, "And I understand you are supposed to meet the jockey tomorrow?" As Napolitano sat with his head down, Donnie stood in front of him fuming. "Never mind for now." A minute passed. Donnie walked back to his desk, looking at Bonaventura squarely in the eye. Bonaventura met the capo's icy look understanding the order. Words were not necessary.

They walked out of the office, and Bonaventura spoke in a rare conciliatory tone, "Bob, what you have to do is get away. Take a trip to Miami. You know everybody there," he suggested. "You, know, maybe for a few weeks until things cool down. I'll square you away with Donnie," said Bonaventura, "The first thing we need to do is get these guys off your tail."

"How are we going to do that?" asked Napolitano.

"Bob, you know the mall in Burlington?"

'You mean the one off Route 128?" asked Napolitano.

"Yeah, that one. You drive there, park as close as you can to the southeast entrance and go in."

"For what?" Napolitano asked.

"We just want to know if the cops are still tailing you. Listen to me," Bonaventura said in an uncommon good-natured voice. "When you go into the mall, there is a men's room right across the way next to the bookstore," he continued. "Go in the men's room. In the back, there's a steel door that opens to the perimeter road behind the mall. Me and a couple of the boys will be right there; we'll jar the door open for you from the outside. You come out and jump in the car."

"What if they still are following behind?" asked Napolitano.

"They won't know where you went when they come inside the mall. We'll drive you home. You throw a few things in a suitcase; I'll take you to the airport." Still with the appeasing voice, Bonaventura said, "Listen to what I tell you; after a few weeks in the sun relaxing you'll come back fresh. The cops will have forgotten about you by then."

"What do I tell my wife? And What about my car?" asked Napolitano.

"Just tell her you have to take a quick business trip out of town. Give no details. The car, you leave it open when you park. One of the boys will drive it back to the warehouse," said Bonaventura, "It'll be all right."

Having followed Donnie's order, there was no Napolitano to meet with Luke the following afternoon.

The morning after the missed appointment, while waiting for a groom to get a horse ready to gallop, Luke sat in the warm tack room and picked up the morning's newspaper lying on the trainer's desk. On the front page, there was a file picture of Robert Napolitano under the headline, "POLICE INVESTIGATE GANGLAND SLAYING IN IPSWICH." The report described in gruesome detail the finding of a body of a man with known Mob connections in a partially hidden marsh on Boston's north shore. He had been hogtied with an electrical cord in the trunk of a Lincoln Town Car and shot in the head.

PART SEVEN

Riled by the events of the past few days, including Napolitano's murder, Luke told his agent that he needed to leave Boston for a while. He had always wanted to try Miami in the winter and thought now was the right time.

Dwyer listened to the young man he had come to admire, not only for his ability as a jockey but also for having his head straight in comparison to other young riders he had known over the years.

"I know an agent in New Jersey who has represented top jockeys in Florida for years. I'll give him a call. Even if he can't take your book right now, I'm sure he'll recommend somebody," said Dwyer.

Luke told his mother of his plans. While his mother didn't know all that had transpired, she knew that something had been worrying her son since the week before. She helped him pack his clothes in the car that night. He planned to get started early the next morning.

It was still dark when Luke and his mother hugged at the door of the house Luke had given her as a birthday present two years before. He told her he'd call once he got settled in Florida.

Luke had dated Caroline Huddleston for nearly a year. As she had planned, she returned to school the previous September, joining her older sister at Mount Vernon College. Luke called her the night before leaving Boston and told her he would stop by her apartment in Washington D.C. for a couple of days before continuing on to Miami. He told her maybe she could come down during one of her breaks from school, to which she quickly agreed, replying, "It'll be great to see you, Luke. What a surprise! You know what? There is a musical I want to see. Maybe we can go while you're here."

"It's a date! I'll see you tomorrow night. You give me the details, and I'll get the tickets," Luke responded.

When Madelaine, the older of the two Huddleston girls, learned that Luke was visiting for two or three days, she told her younger sister she would bunk with a girlfriend from school so that Caroline and Luke could have privacy, as the two sisters shared a small one-bedroom apartment near school.

Upon his arrival, Luke and Caroline ordered Chinese takeout from a restaurant near the apartment. They spent the evening catching up since they hadn't seen each other since the previous summer.

The next morning Caroline had an early class. As she was walking out the door, she asked Luke what he planned to do for the day.

"I was thinking of taking a ride to the racetrack in Laurel and see some friends. I'll stop on the way and get the tickets for Saturday night's show." After a kiss, Caroline left for school, glad to see Luke.

On the way to Laurel, Luke got off the beltway exit and drove to the supper club where a remake of the old Broadway hit "Annie Get Your Gun" was playing.

At the box office, he was told, "Sorry sir, we're sold out, this being the last weekend of this show. We sold out weeks ago."

Walking to his car, Luke thought to himself, *We'll find something else to do. Musicals are not my thing anyway.*

A half hour later, arriving at the Laurel Race Course stable gate, Luke caught sight of his friend Steve Spenser getting into his car. Spenser, like Luke in New England, was winning races at a hot pace in Maryland.

Luke honked his horn, and the two friends hugged and shook hands.

"What the hell are you doing here boy?" Spencer said. "You know you New England guys aren't allowed down here."

"Hey, you know how it is. Everybody can't have it as easy as you," said Luke smiling.

"Look, I'm just going home to change," Spencer told him. "Why don't you follow me? We'll come back; you can get a sandwich in the jocks' room and watch a couple of races. I ride six today."

In the two-bedroom apartment not far away, the two chatted with Luke telling his friend that his girlfriend, Caroline, was going to school in D.C. so he stopped to visit her on his way to Miami.

"Hey, if you're going to be around Saturday night," Spenser offered, "a bunch of us go to this karaoke bar in town and have some laughs. You can bring your girl."

"Actually, we just might take you up on that," said Luke, "She wanted to go to a musical at that place off the beltway, but they told me they were sold out."

"You mean 'Annie Get Your Gun'?"

"Yeah. That's it."

"You know, Luke, it's funny. Like you, I never thought I would like a musical," said Spenser. "I've been messing around with this girl, and we went to see it weeks ago. It was actually very good."

Suddenly, the door opened, and a tall man wearing a fur jacket, with pale skin and jet black hair came in.

"Hey Luke, here is the man who can get you in to see that show," said Spencer. "Meet my agent, Herb Salman."

Luke shook the agent's hand. "So, you are the jock that's going gangbusters in Boston," said Salman in the smooth deep voice that once got him a DJ gig at a radio station in the Midwest. A friend had later told him that on the racetrack, all a hustling man needs is a pencil and a free condition book to become a jockey's agent.

"Now, what's this show you're talking about?" asked Salman.

After listening to jockey Spencer tell of Luke's being turned away at the box office, Salman asked the name of the place as he reached for the yellow pages.

"Watch a master at work," said the agent as he dialed the number after finding it in the phonebook.

"Hello," he said in a fake southern drawl, "Yes dear, what's the name of the person in charge?"

"He's the general manager you say?" replied Salman into the telephone, "Well, then may I speak to Mr. Walker, please? When the person at the other end asked who she should say was calling, Salman floored the two jockeys listening to the conversation when he identified himself.

"Certainly," in his best imitation of a Georgia gentleman, "This is Jodie Powell, calling from the White House for President Carter."
They busted up laughing listening as Salman identified himself as the President's press secretary.

"Yes sir, Mr. Walker," continued Salman with the ruse, "This is Jodie Powell, calling on behalf of President Carter. Yes, sir, of course, yes, thank you for the support. The situation is that the President is hosting a delegation of dignitaries from Spain for the next few days." Salman was just getting warmed up, "The son of one of these gentlemen had an aide call your establishment earlier today and was told your Saturday night show was sold out."

"That being the case, I would greatly appreciate if perhaps you can do anything to accommodate the Spanish Prime Minister's son and his date."

The room went silent as Salman listened to the club's G.M. "Mr. Walker, you're a gentleman, sir. I will tell the President this otherwise crucial issue has been taken care of by your kind understanding and generosity."

That was all it took. As instructed by the man on the phone, Luke was to ask for Mr. Walker upon their arrival at the supper club, and from there all he and an appreciative Caroline had to do was to relax and enjoy the front row table, the show and the nice dinner, champagne included, all compliments of the venue's general manager.

"Always remember Luke, jockey agents are the backbone of the racing industry," Salman declared.

26

After saying goodbye to Caroline two days earlier, Luke arrived in Miami and set out to find a place to live. Friends had told him Hialeah would be the most central to the three racetracks in South Florida.

Fortunately, that same afternoon he found a sparsely furnished apartment on the second floor of a two-story building across the street from the entrance to Hialeah Park, "Well, this is my headquarters for the winter," he said to himself.

The next day, outside the Calder Race Course racing office as previously arranged, he met up with Al Cummings, the jockey agent suggested by Paul Dwyer's friend from New Jersey.

For the past six years, Cummings had been the agent of Ruddy Valor, the leading rider the previous three winters in South Florida. Earlier that year, however, the jockey was severely injured in a spill the last day of Chicago's Hawthorne Race Course meeting. It was feared that the jockey would be paralyzed from the waist down as a result. At first, the agent considered taking some time off to get over the shock of Valor's accident. Then came the call from New Jersey about the possibility of representing Luke Nodarse in Miami that winter.

The agent and jockey made the rounds from barn to barn, introducing Luke to trainers and owners. Except for reading their names in the Morning Telegraph—the Racing Form's sister publication on the East Coast—Luke didn't personally know any of the horsemen he met that morning. He was flattered that some of them were aware of his success in the Northeast, and due to their previous association with riders represented by Cummings, many committed to giving the newcomer a shot on horses in upcoming races. Luke finished the morning by breezing two horses for Karl Stevenson, a personal friend of Cummings who had one of the larger stables at Calder.

It was the first time Luke rode a horse over the much publicized, sand-covered synthetic racetrack designed especially for summer racing at Calder Race Course.

That afternoon Luke met up with his agent at the races, where he was surprised to run into two trainers from Boston who had brought their stables south for the winter. From them, Cummings accepted calls for races for the next entry day.

Already with riding assignments for the next two days, Luke continued to accompany his agent on morning rounds, meeting trainers at Gulfstream and Hialeah, which was due to begin its meeting two days later.

While getting to know his surroundings, he also took the time to enjoy Hallandale Beach, finding the warm water there a far cry from New England beaches where even during summer, the water was always unpleasantly frigid.

He had often read that Hialeah Park was one of the most beautiful racetracks in the world, once seeing its magnificent Renaissance Revival clubhouse, landscaped gardens and pink flamingoes on a small island in its infield lake, Luke understood the accolade. On the first day of the meeting, giddy with anticipation, Luke was named to ride two mounts for one of the trainers from Boston he had seen days earlier. While the first one finished off the board in the third race, the second one finished in a dead heat for the win after a stirring stretch duel with another horse in the sixth race. Luke was on his way.
Riding against world-class jockeys, some surely bound for the Racing Hall of Fame, gave Luke the satisfaction of real accomplishment. Being among them, and getting to know them was the stuff of dreams for the young rider from New England.

Later in the spring, at the conclusion of racing at Gulfstream Park, the other beautiful South Florida facility, Luke finished the winter season with a total of 27 winners. Both he and his agent were satisfied they had done well enough against the tough South Florida jockey colony, and agreed to stay in Miami for Calder's summer meeting to get better acquainted with Florida horsemen and possibly do even better the following winter.

They were right. At Calder, Luke rode more horses regularly. It was a different experience riding over the sand-covered racetrack; it was the first time he saw such a racing surface. At some point after the start of the meet, it was announced that Calder would be closing for the month of August to make necessary repairs and resurface the racing strip. Luke thought he'd take that opportunity to return to Boston for something of a working vacation.
.

27

In 1972, Suffolk Downs added another exotic wager to its betting menu. Called the twin trifecta, the two-dollar bet required players to pick the first three finishers of the seventh race in the exact order, receive a portion of the handle, then exchange the winning ticket for the second half of the wager in the ninth race, where one was required to pick the first three finishers in that race, again in the exact order. If no one correctly picked the two races comprising the twin trifecta, the pool carried over to the next racing day, or until someone accomplished the feat.

The lucrative twin trifecta quickly became the favorite bet for those looking for possible big payoffs, since the more days without winners, the larger the pool became, sometimes into hundreds of thousands of dollars.

"The bet is for suckers," commented jockey Sam Bruno to his pals. "It's hard enough to pick one winner. It's almost impossible to pick six horses to finish just where you need them."

Nevertheless, the big payoffs of the twin trifecta motivated him to think if maybe there was a way to beat the house. After much thought, several days later, the crafty Bruno came up with an idea: "What if you fixed both races?"

Usually, the fields in the two races that involved the twin were made up of more than nine or ten runners. The two races were set up in a way to make it much harder for bettors to pick three correct horses from the larger fields.

In Bruno's mind, the trick would be to wait for races where he knew the jockeys riding would be willing to accept bribes to keep their mounts from hitting the board in each of the two races. In his devious mind, Bruno estimated it would take a six-to-seven-thousand-dollar investment to get the job done.

With Bob Napolitano, his connection for such an operation, found murdered weeks earlier, it was a matter of finding another sucker to finance the caper.

Meanwhile, on the other side of town, the association of Tom Sweeny and Jimmy D'Angelo had evolved into more than a mere acquaintance. Since meeting Jimmy at The Fenway, Tom became a regular, using his low-level celebrity status to entice the unsuspecting coeds who frequented the club.

For his part, Jimmy enjoyed being close to Tom. Not so much because he was fond of the young rider but more for what the jockey was willing to do to stay in favor with Jimmy and his associates at The Fenway.

It had already happened that at Jimmy's request, Tom used drugs and money to entice his jockey pals to play games with their horses, with Southie's Irish Mob benefiting from the shenanigans
.

28

Early one muggy summer morning in 1980, with the Rockingham Park meeting in full swing, horsemen standing along the outer rail of the track watching their charges in training, and the riders on horses on the racetrack noticed what looked like flames of fire emanating from the front side of the grandstand. Within moments, the fire, said to have started in the grandstand's boiler room, engulfed the mostly wooden, 70-plus-year-old building.

Unable to contain the blaze, fire departments from nearby Methuen and Lawrence, Massachusetts, came to the aid of the small, mostly volunteer fire corps of Salem, all to no avail. The fire destroyed the grandstand and clubhouse of the racetrack. After several hours, all that remained of the venerable venue often referred to as the Saratoga of New England was a pile of smoldering rubble. Summer racing in New Hampshire came to an abrupt and sad ending.

Thirty-five miles away in neighboring Massachusetts, shuttered while Rockingham staged the summer racing season, Suffolk Downs quickly switched gears, and with consent from the racing commission, came to the aid of the industry and the local horsemen by committing to finishing out the summer meeting at its facility. By doing so, year-round racing at Suffolk Downs became a reality, as years earlier the Boston racetrack had extended its meeting after the end of thoroughbred racing in Rhode Island's Lincoln Downs in 1976, and Narragansett Park in 1978, due to the loss of customers to a recently opened casino and off-track betting operation in nearby Connecticut.

The public's show of support that summer was amazing. Large crowds attended the improvised summer meeting at Suffolk. The large daily handles ppured money into the mutuel machines, and for the next four weeks the twin trifeta pool continued to grow, as no winning tickets were sold.

The pot was now just under $300,000, to those able to pick the correct win, place and show finishers in the seventh race, and cash and trade their tickets for the first, second and third horses in the ninth race.

PART EIGHT

The voice was raspy and brusque. At 6'2" and grossly overweight his breathing was labored and moving around was a struggle. But it had not been that way years ago when he was flying high living the life of a conniving and prosperous scam artist. His specialty had been rigging races to pull off betting coups. He had done it at small racetracks up and down the East Coast 30 years before. At 61 years of age, this giant of a man had done and seen it all. Now content to take it easy, an Irish gang henchman would drive him to catch a few races every day during the Suffolk meet, and maybe cash a bet. Then, late into the nights, he'd sit in the backroom at The Fenway going over past performances and making marks in the early edition of the Morning Telegraph that he bought as he left the racetrack every afternoon. He was known as Big Al. His opinion of horses and jockeys was respected and relied on by his horse-player associates in the Mob.

For weeks, he had kept an eye toward the rising twin trifecta pool at the track. For the many scores he had managed in his life as a race fixer, none was as substantial as the growing carry-over twin trifecta at Suffolk Downs. Big Al was ready to roll back time and pull off the greatest scheme of all.

"You have to get that punk kid friend of yours to sit down here and listen to me," he said to Jimmy D'Angelo one night pointing at a chair in front of him. "Bring him here and I'll tell him how we're going to hit that twin trifecta gimmick."

The next morning, Jimmy parked his car outside the Suffolk Downs stable gate waiting to see Tom Finney. They drove to a breakfast place not far away from the racetrack where Jimmy told Tom that Big Al had something he wanted to discuss, "Only thing, Al has already run this conversation by the bosses in Southie, and they're on board," said Jimmy. "So listen to him and do as he tells you."

"What is it that he wants?" asked Tom.

"Come by the club tonight and find out," responded Jimmy.

At The Fenway's back office later that night, Tom sat across the table from Big Al listening to what he was being told to do. In a menacing whisper, the large man explained the plan while looking at numbers he had written down on a pad, "What I'm about to tell you, keep it under your hat. No one has to know." He never looked directly at Tom.

I'll tell you when," the heavyset man said, "You gonna have all the money you need to get this done," Al said struggling to catch his breath, "You gonna start low, maybe $500 or $600 to all except the 20 to 1 shots on the program. To the ones riding shorter odds go as far as $2000." For the first time, Al raised his head. Looking straight into Tom's eyes threateningly, he said, "You tell me if anybody turns you down. It will be the greatest mistake that little man will ever make."

Tom assured Al he understood, and that he would get right on it by speaking to his jockey pals. He didn't have a choice. Big Al had given him his marching orders, and he had no option but do as he was told to maintain favor. As he left The Fenway that night, with some hesitation, Tom considered himself the newest confidence man of the Irish Family of gangsters.

30

As previously agreed, Caroline had come to Miami at the start of her summer vacation. Days when Luke had no mounts were spent sightseeing and getting to know the city and the beaches.

One particular afternoon, they found themselves east of Biscayne Bay in a fashionable neighborhood with the catchy name *Coconut Grove*. They walked around going in and out of the trendy shops. In one of them, Caroline bought a yellow cap with a multicolored parrot etched on one side, Luke laughed when she put it on, asserting, "Congratulations, you are now an official New England rube lost in South Florida."

They came upon a French bistro with an interesting menu. Dining was alfresco on checkered cloth-covered tables along the sidewalk each shaded by a colored parasol. One menu item, in particular, caught Luke's attention: *Moules et Frites*. To someone originally from Rhode Island, the entree was simply mussels boiled in a wine broth with a side of French fries. They also ordered a Nicoise salad to accompany the shellfish, which was actually delicious if different. The nice white wine suggested by the manager-waiter complemented the fare.

Done eating, they sat enjoying the last of the bottle while watching the people strolling by, when Luke said, "I don't know if it's the mussels, the wine, or just being here with you. I'm one happy camper."

In silence, they touched hands and looked into each other's eyes, Luke gently toying with her fingertips, when his lips moved. . . .
"What? What did you say?" exclaimed Caroline.

"What, what?" mocked Luke. He got up, went to her, and taking her hands in his, he dropped to one knee and asked, "Will you marry me?"

Customers at nearby tables took it all in and begin clapping and shouting, "Yes! Yes! Yes!"

Blushing and smiling, Caroline nodded her head and said yes.

Hearing the commotion and learning what had transpired, the waiter picked up the empty bottle of wine from the table, looked at it, and in his distinctive French accent said, "They told me this wine was very good, but maybe is better than that; a fresh bottle is on the house, and we see what happens next."

Driving home later that evening, Luke asked her what her father would say when he spoke to him.

"Are you kidding?" she said, "He's forever saying my sister and I are too old to still be living at home," and continued, "He says he and Mom need the closet space."

The following week they flew home to Boston.

It helped that they knew each other. The conversation between Luke and Caroline's father went as expected. The old man said he and his wife were pleased to have Luke as a member of the family. They scheduled a get-together for the following weekend, to meet Luke's mother, his Aunt Lucy and his grandparents. At some point, Luke and Caroline announced that they had decided the wedding would be in May, just nine months away.

As Luke and his family were getting ready to leave the Saturday get-together a week later, Caroline called Luke aside. "I have a surprise for you." For a moment, Luke thought Caroline was going to tell him they were expecting. In Miami, one day when Luke rode the last race at Calder, Caroline went on a tour of the University of Miami, arranged by one of her professors at Mount Vernon, who was an alumna of UM. Caroline had decided on the medical profession. She had applied to two schools in the North East, and took a shot at UM, where she was accepted. The letter had arrived just that morning.

Calder's hiatus that August also allowed Luke to take a drive to the burned down Rockingham Park. While most of his success had come at Suffolk Downs, Rockingham was special to Luke. From the start of his riding career, he would rent a summer cottage in one of the nearby lakes. His mother and Aunt Lucy would come up during their vacations from work. His grandparents, too, came up and stayed two weeks or more. Abuelo enjoyed the races. He had become quite the handicapper and could be found by the Rockingham paddock and the two-dollar windows every racing afternoon. After a time, many of Luke's friends at the track got to know his grandfather.

On summer vacation from school, Caroline and her sister would go up to spend the weekends in New Hampshire. It was funny that the relationship that took root during those lazy summer days, resulted in Luke's and Caroline's impending marriage.

In the four years following the fire, things got complicated for horse racing in New England, as a smaller, more modern grandstand was built on the Rockingham site by new owners with their own management team. However, with Suffolk Downs now staging year-round racing, an intense battle for horses and fans ensued, as the tracks competed head to head. New England racing would never be the same again.

He drove back to Boston that afternoon, stopping by the jockeys' room at Suffolk Downs. His always jovial valet, Cosmo, gave him a big hug. "We've been watching; you're doing all right in Miami."

"Not too bad, the racing there is very different from here. The riding is much tougher against those heavy heads down there."

"Are you going to try riding a few races while you're up here? Cosmo asked.

"Yeah. I'll talk to Paul, see if he can find me a few mounts. It'll be a working vacation so to speak. But the most important part of the trip is that I asked Bruce Huddleston to let me marry his daughter."

"Hey, that's fantastic, Luke. Mazel tov!" exclaimed Cosmo, hugging the jockey.

"Yup, your little brother is off the market, Cos," Luke said with a smile.

PART NINE

By now Sam Bruno was ready to set in motion the plan he had devised. Late one afternoon, he showed up at Angie's Inn and Supper Club, asking to see Nick Rosetti. He was told Nick had not arrived yet.

Bruno hung around the lobby for two hours. It was already dark outside except for the large, multicolored neon sign in front of Angie's, announcing: "One Night Only, Direct from the Dunes Hotel in Las Vegas: DICKEY GREENE'S COMEDY REVUE!"

The large dining room was ready as white table cloths, fresh flower centerpieces and two large overhead clear glass chandeliers welcomed the dinner crowd wearing tuxedos and gowns. The six-member combo on the stage playing old standards was drowned out by the din of the throng of guests being led to their tables by the two maître d's.

In the office upstairs, the 50-something man sitting in front of Donnie was saying, "Vegas is the same, the same routine, the same theater full of people every night. You know, Don, after three months you're just burned out. That's why when Frank suggested I come back east for a while to relax and see family in welcoming surroundings, I decided he was right."

"And we're thrilled to have you, Dickie," said Donnie to the famous comedian. "We sold out as soon as we announced you were coming. We sit about 650, plus another 100 or so standing room only around the bar. The last time we had such a crowd was years ago when Dionne Warwick was here. So we're grateful you accepted the invitation. Oh, the mayor and his entourage will be in the front row, so have some fun with them. Give them the needle."

"I have some stuff especially for politicians. You'll get a kick out of it. By the way, Frank said he was looking forward to your visit to Palm Springs next winter."

"We wanted to go and spend some time, but I don't know, Dickie. There's so much going on here. Sometimes it's tough to get away for any length of time," Donnie confessed. "We'll just have to see. But we will definitely be in Vegas for a few days. We have business there to tend to. Hey, was everything okay with the car and the chauffeur? He picked you up on time?"

"Everything was fine, Don," Greene answered.

"Remember, the place in Cape Cod is all ready for you and your family. You're welcome to use it as long as you want."

"Thank you, thank you," said Greene. "You know, something I'd like to do while I'm in town is go to the races. I always have fun at Suffolk Downs."

"Sure, we can arrange that. We'll set you upstairs in the clubhouse with a couple of the boys to keep the ballbusters away. Management will probably have a race in your name, and you can make the trophy presentation in the winner's circle."

"Thank you so much, again; it's great to get away," said the smiling Greene. "Hey, I should go down and get ready. I have a little ritual I do before going on. It's going to be a great show."

"I have never seen you when you're not great."

Greene took Donnie's hand with both of his. "We'll have a drink later, right?"

"It's our joint. We'll have two drinks!" Donnie said smiling.

As Greene walked out the back way of the office, there was a tap on the front door. One of Donnie's bodyguards walked in wearing formal wear that appeared too tight around the waist, "Boss, that jockey Bruno has been downstairs a while waiting to speak to Nick," he said.

"Is Nicky here yet?"

"No, boss," the man answered. "He called and said he was running a little late."

"Well, you tell Bruno he can't come here and expect to talk to anybody without first calling and making an appointment," Donnie said, waving the man away.

Upon getting the message, Bruno walked to the parking lot mumbling to himself, "Who is he, the President? Call and make an appointment," he muttered. "I come here to cut them into a great score, and get sent away like a dog." He zipped up his jacket against the cool breeze blowing in from the ocean. "Fucking wops, you take away their greasy hair and fancy clothes, and all you have is another dago just off the boat."

32

After making the appointment the following morning, Bruno went to see Nick Rosetti. The meeting took place in Donnie's upstairs office. Donnie and Babe Bonaventura also sat in wondering what the old jockey had to say.

"I have a proposition for you," said Bruno. "Have you guys been paying attention to the increasing pot of the twin-tri at Suffolk? It's already over $300,000."

The three men kept quiet listening to where the conniver was going.
"I've come up with a sure way to hit it," Bruno said proudly. "You know, to win the money means you have to pick the first three finishers in two races."

They remained silent, as Bruno continued to explain his plan.

"I figure I can tie up both races. You know, pay off the jockeys to hold their horses so the numbers we pick are the only ones to hit the board."

At this point, Nick glanced at Donnie. Bonaventura kept his eyes on Bruno.

"Now, the field of both these races are anywhere from nine to twelve horses," Bruno continued. "I think the operation will cost eight to ten grand to pull off." He sat still waiting for a response.

After a moment of continued silence, Donnie spoke first, "And you come to us to foot the bill."

"Well, yeah. I don't have that kind of money laying around, you know," Bruno responded, and continued, "But look at it this way, the winnings will go to you."

There was no quick reaction. They knew that Bruno had been Bob Napolitano's inside man to fix races in the past. True, most of the time a set up took place they walked away winners. Including the time when Bruno dropped the young bug boy when they scored over $160,000.

Again, Nick looked at Donnie, reading what was on his mind. He turned and said to Bruno, "You say the winning will go to us, so what is in it for you?"

"Well, I would hope a substantial piece since it was my idea."

Nick pondered the answer, replying, "Look, Bruno, we have to talk this over before we can give you an answer either way."

"What's there to talk about? Either you're in or not." With his impetuous display, Bruno hit a nerve.

Donnie moved forward in his chair, and glared into Bruno's eyes, "If you need an answer right now, well, the answer is we're not interested. If you want to get back to us in a day or two like you were told that could change. Furthermore, you're a fresh little bastard, and since this is the first time I set eyes on you, I will tell you I don't like you. You don't come into my house demanding answers with an attitude. A taller man would leave here with his legs broken!"

Bruno cringed in his chair.

"Like I said, you can get in touch with Nick in a day or two. For now, this meeting is over." Donnie stood up, clearly angry, "Get out!"

The room went still as Bruno got up and left the office without another word.

Shit, I think I fucked up, Bruno thought to himself as he drove away. No one had ever confronted him the way Donnie Giordano did. The best he could hope for was that Donnie cooled off in a couple of days when Bruno tried to contact Nick again.

The next day, as they were getting ready to go out to supervise other parts of their operation, Nick asked Donnie, "What about that guy Bruno?"

Donnie responded while putting on his sweater, "I don't know. What are you thinking?"

"Donnie, I don't trust this guy; I think it's a pass."

"You know, I've always told you we think alike," a slight smile on his face, "We're supposed to give the guy ten grand, come up with the betting money, and let him pick the horses? What does he think? We came around yesterday? Look, Nick, I've come to realize the best advice I've received in a long time was my uncle telling me to get out of the horse racing racket years ago."

Nick nodded.

"We have far too many things going on. We need to be in Vegas next week to look at this Dunes casino business. They expect a firm commitment. We really don't need the heat that Bruno's race fixing scheme will probably generate. If he calls back, tell him we're not interested; let him take his business to the guys in Southie. They are his people anyway, aren't they?"

It was agreed. They would pass on Bruno's plan.

33

It was before sunrise when jockey Tony Suarez drove his car through the Suffolk Downs stable and took his assigned parking spot behind barn 12. As he opened the trunk to reach for his boots and helmet, he heard a voice,

"What do you say, brother-in-law?" A startled Suarez turned around to see Tom Sweeny walking toward him.

"Hey man, why do you always call me that?" Suarez asked.

"You forget? I've seen your sister."

"You're not her type. She likes her boyfriends tall and muscular."
"Hey, I'm muscular." They both laughed. "Seriously, I need to talk to you. Let's get back in the car." Tom walked around and got in the passenger's side.

"What's up?" asked Suarez.

"Listen, you ride a horse in the seventh race tomorrow."

"Yeah, *Hardwick Hall*, Arnason's horse," Suarez said.

"Anyway," Tom continued, "what if I give you 800 not to finish 1-2-3 in the race?" he said reaching into his pocket.

Tony Suarez looked at Tom pondering what his friend was asking him to do. Seconds passed. "Hey, I'll try my best," he said, "I don't like that Englishman trainer anyway."

Tom held the money in his hand, "Never mind your best. It's got to happen." He laid the eight 100-dollar bills on Tony's seat, asking, "What about the horse you ride for the same guy in the last race?"

"You mean *Royal Upset*, shit Tom, that horse will win," Suarez asserted. "He got into all kinds of trouble in his last start."

"Will you take $2000 for that one?" Tom asked.

"I don't know, Tom. Like I said, that horse will win. Shit, he's the favorite in the race."

"Yeah, and you'll make, what? Just over $200 for winning?" Tom argued, "I'm offering you ten times that much … Besides, you said you don't like the trainer anyway."

Suarez pondered, and came back, "What about $2300?" he asked.

"What's this, Let's Make a Deal? Take $2200, and tell your sister I want to marry her."

"That will be the day. I'll see you later," Suarez said as they went in different directions.

"One down," Tom thought to himself.

At the door of the track kitchen, Tom looked around for the next victim. At a table with his back to a wall, he spotted Rick Willis sitting with a couple of guys Tom didn't know. Getting Willis' attention, he motioned him out with a nod.

Outside, Willis asked, "What duyo want. You want to say you are sorry for shutting me off in the last race last night?

"Forget about that. I told you the horse was lugging in. Let's walk toward the parking lot," Tom said. "Where's your truck?"

Willis answered by pointing to his vehicle parked four cars away. Once inside the truck, Tom offered the jockey $700 to hold the horse he rode in the seventh race the following day.

"Hell, is that all there is?" Willis asked taking another drag from his cigarette.

"The horse is 12 to 1. He ain't going nowhere," Tom pointed out, "I just need to be sure that by some act of God he doesn't finish second or third; that's why I'm paying you."

By the end of the morning, Tom had engaged eight jockeys toward the 14 he needed to pay off for both races. That afternoon, in the jockeys' room, he got the other six, using up the $10,000 front money Big Al had given him.

That night, at The Fenway, Tom told Big Al the job had been completed. According to Al's calculations for the seventh race, numbers 3-5-8, all at least 15 to 1 odds in the morning line, and surely much higher at post time, will make up the first trifecta, and after that, exchange the ticket for another box in the ninth race, using the numbers 1-3-7. No matter what place the three horses finish would bring them the over $300,000 twin-trifecta. Big Al sat back on his chair, proud to have put it all together. The old race fixer had not lost his touch.

For his part, Bruno still couldn't believe the Italians had passed up on his idea to fix the Suffolk's twin trifecta. For a second, he again blamed himself for the bad presentation, "Shit, I thought I was meeting with Nick alone. It was that fucking Donnie that put the squash on the whole thing." But Bruno was not deterred. *This is too good a way to make real money*, he thought to himself as he drove toward Boston. *I'm sure the Irish will go along with the idea.*

"Is Jimmy around?" Bruno asked the bartender setting up behind the counter as he walked in the door of The Fenway.

"Oh, he's not in yet."

"What about Big Al?" asked Bruno.

"He's in the back," answered the man.

He tapped on the door before entering. Sitting at the usual table with his tip sheets and notepad with numbers written on it in the dimly lit room, Big Al looked up at Bruno and nodded his head.

"What's going on Al? Long time no see," said Bruno.

Al grunted. "Where have you been?"

"I've been busy. Been helping this guy in Rhode Island," Bruno responded not sure why the lie. "He's got some horses down there that I don't think will ever make it to the track, but he's paying me good money."

Big Al looked down, as if not listening.

"Hey Al, what about that tri at Suffolk?" said Bruno faking enthusiasm. "I was thinking maybe we can make a play for it, you know, fix those damned races and get the money."

Silence engulfed the room.

After a few moments, Big Al said, "Bruno, I'm just too damned old to go back and get involved anymore. My days of big schemes and big scores are over," he said in a raspy voice, "I'm content with just sitting here trying to pick a winner now and then just to keep a hand in the game."

"Come on Al, I have it all figured out," said Bruno, almost pleading, "You get your guys from Southie to put up the few bucks it will take, and we can hit this thing."

"Look, I'm out. You can stay here, kibitz, and have a cup of coffee with me, or go and find someone else interested in your idea. But I'm out.

A half hour later, a crestfallen Sam Bruno walked out into the bright sunshine, understanding that this would not be his big shot, his grand score. It was at that moment he realized his scheming days were over. "I'm yesterday's news," he said to himself.

34

In the track kitchen, Luke sat chatting with two old clients. One of them, Bob Kelly, had saddled the winner that put Luke on top of the jockey standings at Suffolk months earlier.

"If I had known you were going to be here I would have put you on the two I have in today," said Kelly.

"Ah thanks, but I'm only here visiting, and spending some time with my family. I'll be going back to Miami in few days," Luke confessed.

Just then, Luke's old agent Paul Dwyer, came in to find him at the table with the two horsemen. "Hey Luke, come with me. I want to introduce you to a trainer that's looking for a rider for a horse he has in tomorrow."

"Excuse me, guys. Paul just can't accept that I'm just visiting," Luke said smiling as he went to meet his agent.

Walking out of the kitchen, Dwyer explained, "This trainer, Ralph Arnason, has a stable of nice horses. He brought his own rider from Canada, but the jockey was injured in a race the first week after arriving in Boston. He's been using Suarez, but he can't ride him. He has call on another horse in the race."

The trainer spoke with a slight British accent. He walked Luke and Dwyer to a stall to see the horse Luke was to ride, as the bay horse leisurely picked at the hay rack in front of the stall, aware of the men coming his way.

In front of the stall, the horse nibbled at the trainer's jacket looking for a treat while the man gently fussed with the animal's ears, "Ah, I have nothing for you today, you big baby," he said to the horse.

"This is *Tudor Knight*," said trainer Arnason. "Mr. Morris, the owner, is a professor of history back home and is a great fan of the English Tudor period, he names all his home-breds with names that relate to that era." He paused, patting the horse, "This one is a gentle horse, easy to ride. Like I told Paul, I think he'll win tomorrow."

After ten minutes, Luke thanked the trainer for the mount once again, as he and Paul walked out and away from the barn.

The next morning, as Luke arrived at the jockeys' room carrying his riding tack in the leather valise his Aunt Lucy had given him the Christmas before, three men from the south end of town were driving on the way to the track. As Big Al had said, they were to buy five $2-dollar trifecta box each, using numbers 3-5-8. This way, they'd be winners as long as those horses finish first, second or third, in any order.

"Hey, Luke," a smiling Cosmo said taking the bag from the young man. "You couldn't stay away; I knew it," he said, ruffling the jockey's hair.

"You know Paul's motto, 'If there's a horse to ride, you ride him'," Luke quipped.

From the other side of the room, Tom Sweeny yelled, "Hey Luke, did they kick you out of Miami?" He laughed as he walked to shake Luke's hand.

"What you been up to, man; knocking them dead?" Luke said.

"You know me; I hold my own," Tom said, undressed with a towel wrapped around his waist, shower slippers dragging on his feet as he walked. "I'll see you later. I have a couple of pounds to pull in the hot box," Tom said.

Several other jockeys came to say hello to their fellow rider. From behind the counter of the jockeys' room cafeteria, Gino, the cook, yelled, "Hey Luke, I have the ciambotta that you like!"

"Hello, Gino. Serve me up a dish. I'll be right over." To his friends, he said, "Come on guys; I'm buying."

The three men were only the first team. Another group was made up of waitresses from The Fenway, also sent by Al, to make the same five transactions at different tellers.

The night before, Al had called bookmakers in Chicago and Kansas City to make the bets he was sure wouldn't come back to the track. He knew his contacts well. That they were old friends from Al's race-fixing days all those many years ago was of no consequence. Friendships end when it comes to money, it was understood.

By post time on the afternoon of the race, every criminal element from the south side of Boston was at the track to bet the same six lucky numbers and witness Big Al's plot come to fruition.

Sam Bruno, hanging around the betting ring looking for a mark to tout, took notice of all the Irish gang members, and wondered if he had been cold watered by Al.

As programmed, the seventh race of the day was the first half of the twin trifecta. Tom's mount in the race, Berry Purple, was a 6 to 1 shot, that would finish off the board as planned. One horse had scratched earlier that morning, leaving six jockeys in the race to hold their mounts back, allowing Big Al's picks, the three horses with the longest odds, to finish 1-2-3.

The grandstand and clubhouse were packed. Saturdays were always busy days at Suffolk, but with the possible record-breaking twin trifecta pot, even more so. Everybody was looking to win the large prize.

"Riders Up!" Called the paddock judge as the jockeys were legged up by their mounts' trainers. Wearing a spiffy red riding coat and black velvet skull-cap, the outrider led the horses on their way to the track for the post parade with the crowd roaring in excitement.

As the warm-up period ended over eight minutes later, the horses filed in order on the way to the starting gate. In the grandstand, the crowd was excited in anticipation.

"It is now post time," bellowed the loudspeakers, as the announcer called out the names of each horse as assistant starters led them to their positions in the starting gate. It was a distance race, with the starting gate situated at the one-sixteenth of a mile marker in front of the grandstand. The throng of fans drew near the outside fence to take in the action up close.

There was a momentary pause as the starter, perched in his stand over the track, quickly assessed all horses were standing ready to be dispatched, the jockeys crouched on their backs.

"They are off!" called the track announcer from his booth atop the grandstand.

As the gates slammed open, aboard #7 *Hardwick Hall,* jockey Tony Suarez fell back on his saddle pulling back on the reins, causing his mount to throw his head back leaving the barrier, to be in last position entering the clubhouse turn.

The field took the turn. Normally, in distance races, jockeys steady their mounts early to reserve speed for when needed later in the race. So it was nothing out of the ordinary to see jockeys raising up on their saddles at this juncture.

They made their way to the backstretch, with all but three jockeys still up on their saddles restraining their mounts as the field scattered, with several lengths between the first and last horse.

In the stewards' stand, two officials watched the race through their binoculars, as a third one intently kept his eyes on the several monitors recording the race from different angles. The field reached the midway point with most jockeys still not moving on their mounts. "Are you guys seeing this?" asked the chief steward to his two colleagues. "It sure looks like they're allowing those three in front to have the race to themselves," said a second steward.

Along the far turn, the same three longshots made the pace while others started to make up ground but still under their riders' restraint. Tom Sweeny was clearly tugging on the reins, keeping his mount from closing in on the leaders.

The scattered field entered the stretch, with the same three horses in front, with some of the trailing horses clearly wanting to run, even as the riders pulled back on their reins.

They passed the finished line, #8 *Sam's Club* at odds of 50 to 1, finished a head in front of the #3 *Itty Bitty* at 33 to 1. Five lengths back, #5 *Cool Moore* at 17 to 1 finished third, one half-length in front of #6 *Hardwick Hall,* the 6 to 5 favorite, with Tony Suarez awkwardly restraining his mount.

In the grandstand, the Southie Mob attempted to appear subdued, downplaying the success of the first half of their scheme. In the stewards' stand, the chief steward picked up the phone and placed a call. "Mutuels Department," the man answered.

"Mitch, this is the stewards. We need you to go over the betting pattern printouts, see if anything jumps out at you. I'm sending state police lieutenant Rodgers down to you. Call us back as quickly as possible."

In the winner's circle, the connections of the winning horse were slapping high fives. It was the horse's first win in a year. In his last eight starts, the horse had finished far back racing against similar competition.

"Judge, it's Mitch. All I see are two-dollar bets, nothing higher. One thing looks odd, though. Most of the bets leave out the favorites in the race, using the first three finishers exactly," reported the mutuels manager.

After pondering the situation rapidly, the stewards decided to make the race official and allow the state police detail assigned to the racing commission to investigate the race.

The payoffs were posted. The winner, #8 *Sam's Club*, paid $118.40 for a two-dollar win ticket; #3 *Itty Bitty*, $37.00, and the show horse, #5 *Cool Moore* returning $22.80 for every two-dollars bet. The two-dollar trifecta was worth a whopping $3102.40.

As soon as he unsaddled his horse and checked his weight on the scale, Suarez sprinted back to the jockeys' room as the angry crowd around the paddock fence heckled and jeered the jockey: "Suarez, you stink, you thief!" "Go back to where you came from, you bum!"

Ralph Arnason, who had watched the race in his box seat with Mr. Morris, the owner of *Hardwick Hall,* rushed to the paddock to speak to Suarez, only to find the jockey had already entered the jockeys' room. He quickly went in the paddock office and dialed the stewards' phone. "Judge, this is Ralph Arnason," the ire in his British accent more pronounced than ever. "I'm certain you witnessed the way my horse was ridden in this race."

"Mr. Arnason," replied the chief steward, "We have already started an investigation, and measures will be taken, I assure you."

"I understand, your honor," Arnason said, harnessing his anger, "Will you please allow me to change riders on my horse in the last race? I'm not so sure that I want to face Suarez under the circumstances."

The steward relayed the request to his fellow officials. "Whom do you want to put on your horse?" the steward asked.

"Luke Nodarse rides for me in this next race," Arnason replied. "I'd like to use him."

Within moments, the stewards called the jockeys' room and requested to speak to Nodarse. "Luke, Ralph Arnason wants to put you on his horse in the last race," the steward continued, "Will you ride him?"

"Absolutely, yes sir."

At the start of the six-furlong eighth race, *Tudor Knight* broke in front under Luke's urging and thereafter made each phase of the race a winning one. A calmer Ralph Arnason helped his elderly owner, Mr. Morris, into the winner's circle to have his picture taken with his horse and a smiling Luke on the saddle. The travesty of the previous race was temporarily forgotten.

When Tom heard of the replacement of riders for the last race, he became agitated. "Shit, this is the worst thing that could happen," he said to himself.

He pulled Suarez into the dark sleeping room in the jockeys' quarters, and after making sure they were alone, he asked, "What the fuck happened?"

"Luke, I told you I was going to have a hard time holding that horse. Hell, it was a terrible exhibition. I did everything but fall off not to finish third. The stewards already called me to their office tomorrow morning."

When Luke returned to the jockeys' room after winning the eighth race, Tom quickly went to him and whispered, "I need to talk to you."

Tom motioned Luke to follow him to the sleeping room, and again after making sure they were alone said, "Luke, this horse you picked up in the last race,"

"What about him?" Luke asked with a creased brow.

"Listen, I'll give you five thousand not to let him hit the board."

Luke bit the side of his lip and cast a stern look into Tom's eyes. He shook his head and walked away without saying a word.

"Luke, I ride the race. If you don't listen to me, I'm going to hurt you out there!"

Luke stopped and turned around. With his face nose to nose with Tom's, in a low and menacing voice, he said, "The problem with you is that you can't understand that I don't give a shit about you or your dirty schemes." Again, he turned and walked away, leaving Tom standing there.

35

When the horses arrived in the paddock for the ninth race, the jockeys lined up to be weighed out by the clerk of scales.
Several minutes later, the clerk urged on the microphone, "Let's go for the last race riders."

In the paddock, the jockeys received last minute instructions from their mounts' trainers. Arnason shook Luke's hand, and once again congratulated him for a great ride in the previous race. "This horse is a little different," he said. "He has early speed if you want to use it, but we've found out his best races are sitting just behind the pacesetters, you know, not rushing him early."

"Mr. Arnason, there's really no speed in this race," said Luke.

"I know, lad. Like I said, he can show speed if you want to use it," the trainer advised, "Look, you ride your own race, however it develops."

"Riders up!" The call was given for riders to mount their horses. Arnason legged up his jockey, and said, "Good luck, both of you," patting the horse's rump.

In the post parade, Luke told the accompanying pony rider to just let the horse walk.
As the field of horses started their way to the starting gate, Luke instructed the pony to take a loose hold of the lead strap. "I got him," Luke said, taking control of the horse.

"Now, let's do a quick sprint to the four and a half, turn around, and do the same thing on the way back to get in line."

The pony rider did as Luke instructed. As they galloped at a quick pace, Luke took a strong hold of the reins, with three quick cracks of his whip on his mount's shoulder. He clucked to the horse making him take hold of the bit and responded by shaking his head fighting the rider's restraint wanting to run on.

They turned around and did the same on the way up to their place in line, with Luke continuing to tap his whip on his mount's shoulder, but restraining the horse, the animal now clearly on the muscle. By the time the assistant starter took a hold of him, the horse was prancing and anxious to run.

The bell rang, and the doors sprang open. Away from the #7 stall, Luke strapped the horse several times to get him on the bit. The urging from the rider quickly put *Royal Upset* in the lead on the backside gradually dropping in toward the rail. Luke took a peek under his left arm and saw Tom riding hard to catch up to him.

Past the half-mile pole, Luke continued to inch toward the inside rail. Three-quarters of a length back, Tom had no other alternative than to try to catch the leader from the inside.

"I'm going to drop that sonobitch," said Tom, himself riding hard to catch Luke.

As they approached the far turn, Luke looked under his left arm again. He saw the head of Tom's horse approaching. Suddenly, and unexpected by Tom, Luke pulled on his left rein shifting his mount farther toward the rail. Thinking he was going to be shut off, Tom raised up on the saddle and yanked his mount back to avoid clipping the heels of Luke's horse. But Luke knew exactly what he was doing, he didn't totally take away Tom's racing room; he merely let him think he was. By Tom taking back, *Royal Upset* and Luke opened up a three-length lead entering the turn and continued widening into the homestretch. Big Al's three horses, giving chase to finish ahead of all the other horses, passed the finish line second, third and fourth, with *Royal Upset*, winning by five lengths and Tom finishing fifth.

Pulling up after the race, Tom rode his horse next to Luke's, and with an angry look, said, "I'm going to get you disqualified, you sonobitch." Luke smiled, and slowly galloped his horse back to the winner's circle.

After unsaddling, Tom rushed toward the scale room, and as he weighed in, said to the clerk, "I want to claim foul against the winner," handing his saddle to his valet at the same time.

The clerk of scales reached for the wall phone to the stewards, "Judge, Tom Sweeny wants to lodge an objection. Here he is," the clerk said, handing the phone to Tom.

The loudspeaker blared, "Ladies and gentlemen, please hold all tickets! The stewards have posted the inquiry sign, and jockey Tom Sweeny, aboard #3 *Move It*, the unofficial fifth place finisher, has lodged a claim of foul against the unofficial winner #7, *Royal Upset*, and jockey Luke Nodarse, for alleged interference entering the far turn. Please hold all tickets while the stewards review the films."

Gasping for air, Tom said into the phone, "Judge, Luke nearly dropped me going into the turn. I had to take up, taking all the momentum away from my horse. There was no reason for him to angle in so sharply."

"We're looking at it. Put Nodarse on," said the chief steward.

Entering the winners' circle, Luke jumped off his mount and went to the phone. "What happened entering the turn?" asked the steward.

"Sir, Tom tried to go where there was no room, he should ha
ve known better."

"Okay, we're looking at it." In the stewards' stand, the three judges watched the monitors playing different angles of the incident in the far turn. One of them said, "It was already tight when Sweeny started up in there."

The chief stewards said, "At the very best there was some degree of intimidation from the seven horse, but Sweeny knows better than to try to get through like he did. We can't disqualify an easy winner to place him fifth, there is no evidence that Sweeny was going to beat Nodarse anyway. The three stewards were in agreement: No disqualification."

The announcement came over the loudspeakers, "Attention ladies and gentlemen. The stewards find insufficient reason to change the order of finish." Within seconds, the red inquiry/objection sign on the infield tote board was replaced by the word "official."

With that, Tom's last-minute attempt to bring success to his malicious intentions failed. Had the stewards disqualified the winner, Tom would have been placed fourth, and Big Al's numbers would have been moved up accordingly to finish first, second and third. But it was not to be.

In the winners' circle, Luke posed with the owner and trainer to have his picture aboard *Royal Upset*. In short order, the crowd went wild as the prices on the board lit up. At 3 to 1 *Royal Upset*, paid $8.40 to win, but you could hear a pin drop when the announcer was heard: "Attention ladies and gentlemen. There are two twin trifecta winners. . . . The payoff for the combination 7-1-3 is . . ." The announcer paused, creating drama as the numbers went up on the tote board, "$420,600.80!"

The record payoff was divided between the two winning ticket holders.

The horse's name, *Royal Upset*, best described the failure of Big Al's careful planning. The Irish Mob's attempt to fix the race had failed. Immediately after the race was made official, the stewards called the jockeys' room and summoned all the riders who rode the race to their office the following morning. State police troopers were already guarding both doors of the jockeys' room. Luke Nodarse was excused.

36

Across the Mystic River from Boston was the city of Chelsea. It's Mill Hill section was a largely residential area consisting mostly of two- and three-story wood frame detached buildings. There, on the second floor of a three-decker, was the home of self-employed plumber Joe Burke and his family. Just over the line from Revere, it was a blue-collar enclave.

Times were tough, but by working hard taking on any job available, Joe was able to provide a good, if simple, life for his wife and two children.

On rare good weeks, he would take Linda, the older of his children, and Larry, two years younger, to Suffolk Downs. These trips provided the youngsters a respite from their gray, drab neighborhood. These were the few times they saw green grass, and they loved the horses.

The father taught them to read the racing program. Sometimes, he would bet two dollars on their selection. They nearly never won; the outings were mostly a way to spend time with his two children.

Linda was petite, with a pretty face and short hair. Her father doted on her. Larry was tall and lanky, a good athlete who could always be found playing street hockey with his pals during the winter, and stick ball or shooting baskets in better weather.

Upon graduation from high school, the parents encouraged Linda to enroll in community college, as she always talked about becoming a nurse.

Two years into her studies at Suffolk County Community College, she was invited to a friend's birthday party. There, she met a tall, strapping, young man. His dark hair was long in the style of the day. He kidded her that his hair was longer than hers was. After the party, he walked her home.

Their frequent dates grew into a real relationship. One month before her twentieth birthday, and against her parents' pleas, she married the young man.

They moved into a one-and-half bedroom apartment in the attic of a two-story home several blocks from her parents. Within a month, she was pregnant.

A baby boy was born, and things were going along well; the grandparents loved the baby, and in time, started to accept Linda's husband.

By now she had left school, working the late shift at a 24-hour pharmacy downtown. Her husband worked in a cardboard box manufacturing company in Chelsea's aptly named Box District.

They often argued about the husband's frequent Friday night get-togethers with his pals from work at a neighborhood tavern. They had been married two-and-half years, and Linda became pregnant again.

More and more, she began to realize her parents had been right. Her first son was a three-year-old toddler, and now she had a new baby with little support from her husband. In his way of thinking: "Kids are the mother's responsibility."

Even with two salaries, they begin to fall back on bills. The landlord had warned that if they didn't pay on time, they would need to find somewhere else to live.

"Hey, it wouldn't hurt your parents to chip in a little. . . . They are their grandkids after all!" said the husband.

More and more the couple grew apart. His weekends were usually spent with his friends watching sports on TV at the tavern. Often, he would come home late at night, drunk and looking for something to eat.

Unable to read the signs of failure, Linda became pregnant yet again two years later, just about the time her husband left for work one morning, never to return again.

Now with three small kids and no husband, she applied for welfare and food stamps. She supplemented the government's aid by cleaning houses for neighbors.

During summer, her mother who lived three blocks away, looked after the kids while Linda went about her chores. One Friday evening, having a family dinner at her mother's house, Linda's younger brother said he was going to the horseraces with his girlfriend the following day. The young man said they had a twin trifecta carryover of over $300,000. Hitting the bet, "would take care of me," he mocked.

As dinner ended, while her father played with the kids in the living room and her mother put away the dishes, Linda went to her purse and took out two crumpled one dollar bills.

She said to her brother, "Here, Larry, play two dollars for me."

"You mean in the twin trifecta? Are you feeling lucky? Tell me what numbers?"

Without much thought, she said, "Use my kids ages; three, five and eight."

"Those are good numbers," said Larry, "Give me three more numbers in case you get really lucky and have to turn over your ticket to get the big prize in the last race."

Momentarily stumped, she thought about it," How about the month and day I was born, March 17. Yeah, that's it; three, one, seven.

By late afternoon the next day Linda had forgotten about her brother's trip to Suffolk Downs. While giving her baby a bath, there was a loud knocking on her door. Linda came running from the bathroom wearing her terrycloth robe, "Who is it?'

"It's me, Larry."

Linda opened the door, said she had the baby in the tub, and hurried back to the bathroom.

Standing in the doorway of the bathroom as his sister rinsed her three-year-old daughter, cool as cucumber, Larry said, "I'm going to show you what a good brother I am. Look what I brought you. Come here."

As she wrapped the baby in a towel, she followed her brother to the bedroom, where he proceeded to empty his jacket and pants pockets, throwing over $200,000 dollars on the bed.

"Ah, ah, ah, ah!" Linda screamed, joyously jumping up and down as the baby in her arms laughed along unable to understand why her mother was so happy.

37

On the airplane back to Miami, Luke read the reports in the Boston Globe, "AUTHORITIES INVESTIGATE BETTING IRREGULARITIES AT SUFFOLK DOWNS" was the headline, the article that followed, "FBI investigates attempted fixing of a sporting event," included an aerial photo of the racetrack.

Putting himself in the middle of the scandal, and wanting to get even for being left out of what could have been a successful coup, Sam Bruno blew the whistle to the cops and was eventually granted immunity for taking part in previous race fixings. In exchange, he would be the star witness for the prosecution, and name the culprits and the illicit events surrounding the twin trifecta at Suffolk Downs. At the conclusion of the trial, he would be placed in the witness protection program.

For his protection, meanwhile, Bruno was moved from his little apartment in Revere to a safe house 60 miles south of Boston.

The FBI team in charge of the investigation included Thomas Morrison, the corrupt agent on the Giordano family payroll. As soon as it became known that Bruno was to testify in exchange for immunity, Morrison placed a call to Donnie at Angie's.

As Bruno slept three nights later, on the second floor of a house at the end of a street in the city of New Bedford, his bedroom door broke open. Before he could get up, accompanied by two other men, Babe Bonaventura forced a gun into Bruno's mouth, "If you mention the Giordano name in any way, I don't care where they hide you; I will find you. Do you understand?" Bonaventura's eyes glared as he wiped the barrel of his thirty-eight special on Bruno's chest. The two-guard detail assigned to the protection of the prosecution's star witness were previously warned to take a walk and not look back.

With Bruno's assistance, 32 indictments were issued by the federal grand jury, including all the jockeys involved plus an assortment of Southie's hoodlums and the heads of their gang. Five days after his indictment as the mastermind of the race-fixing scheme, Big Al O'Donnell died of a massive heart attack. In the months that followed, The Fenway nightclub was forced to close down after its liquor license was revoked by authorities.

The trial lasted two years, but as the numerous appeals ran their course, it took nearly four years for 28 of the originally indicted 32, to begin prison terms of 24 months to 15 years.

The concern of most jockeys is their weight. After five years of riding in the South Florida circuit, Luke was among the leading riders. With Caroline about to graduate from medical school, everything but his increasing weight problem was going well. It was to be expected. He had always watched how much he ate. But lately, his morning soft boiled egg and slice of toast with black coffee was the only food he could sustain without worrying. The problem of his increasing weight forced Luke to spend an hour or two daily reducing in the hot box.

One morning after training, Luke accepted an invitation from a trainer to go to Ocala to check on the progress of the man's several two-year-olds that would be joining his stable in Miami in the next month or two.

Lars Skinner had become a good friend. He had met him two years earlier when Luke's agent introduced him to the trainer, who after spending a few years looking after turnouts at his place in central Florida, decided to come back to the racetrack to start training horses again.

With a 20-horse stable, Skinner kept Luke busy. His barn was where Luke started his daily rounds. He'd get on one or more horses, and then go on to check with other clients. On easy mornings, Luke would visit with Skinner at the barn and chat about racing.

Since meeting Skinner, Luke had wondered why the trainer left the racetrack and retreated to Ocala. He had heard rumors but didn't really know what had happened to a man who had always done well, to leave his stable and Miami and just walk away.

Straying from their conversation about racing, Luke asked, "How come you quit training for all that time?"

Sitting on a folding chair rolling up the white standing bandages, Skinner thought for a moment before responding, "Luke, my wife galloped all of our horses. One day, the horse she was on spooked from a loose horse running the wrong way on the racetrack, and she got thrown into the outside fence," the trainer paused. "Anyway, she was severely injured and spent a few months in the hospital down here. When they let her out I decided to take her back home to the farm to recuperate. I told my owners to look for other trainers. I just left."

Without thinking, Luke asked, "Where is she now?"

Not looking up from rolling the bandages, Skinner answered, "She died three years ago."

"I'm sorry, Lars. I didn't mean too—"

"No, it's all right Luke," Skinner interrupted. "She didn't feel well one evening. I took her to the hospital, and she never returned home. Things happen." It was as if Skinner needed to let out his grief.

38

As they laid in bed one night, Caroline was going over some notes from a class that day while Luke looked at the ceiling lost in thought. "What are you thinking about, honey?" she asked.

"Today, I rode with Lars to Ocala to pick up three of his babies," he said. "You know, Caroline, I think a little place up there with a few acres to keep some horses would be a nice place for us to live." He turned to her to see her reaction.

"Luke, when I married a horseman, I knew there were certain things I would have to go along with," she said. "Remember, I grew up with a horseman. I saw my mother putting up with things because of dad's business, sometimes wishing things were different."

"What are you saying?" Luke wondered.

"Look, my residency at Baptist's ends soon," she explained. "You know that I've looked into several medical groups down here to join once that's done."

"So?" he asked.

"If you find 'a little place' as you call it, up north, I'll look into medical groups up there and we'll move. I want you to be happy."
He moved closer, took the notebook from her setting it aside, and passionately, he kissed her.

Since his conversation with Caroline about central Florida, quitting riding came into the equation. Luke looked into other things he could do within racing.

Going to horse sale events ever since coming to Florida, he enjoyed the goings on as buyers and sellers went about their business. Hanging around with Lars Skinner during those occasions, he had learned a lot about that side of the racing industry.

Skinner told him how he spent his time in Ocala while his wife was recuperating after her accident. "I did some 'pin hooking,' you know, buying yearlings, overseeing their breaking and training and eventually reselling them at a profit as race ready two-year-olds in training," he explained. "Matter of fact, I did the same with a couple of weanlings I bought from a guy getting out of the business. I kept them for a while and sold them later on."

"How did you do?"

"Hey Luke, it's like anything else; there's money to be made if you're willing to work at it," said Skinner.

That night, Luke told his wife of his idea of what to do if he quit riding.

"All you have to do now is find a few acres up there," she said shrugging her shoulders. "We'll do like trees and leave."

You gotta love her, thought Luke taking her into his arms.

So began the search for a small farm.

Two months later, with Caroline having finished her residency at Baptist Hospital, and actively looking for a job in the general area of Ocala, Luke made an appointment to look at a place for sale just north of Ocala's horse country the following weekend.

Earlier that same week, a new owner from New York sent three horses to Lars Skinner. According to their past performances, two of them seemed like they would suit well in South Florida. The third was a three-year-old colt yet to make his first start in a race. In the accompanying envelope containing the foal certificates and veterinarians' reports was a note from the previous trainer: "The colt is green, needs more schooling in the paddock."

After a couple of days of easy galloping, Lars got permission from the paddock judge to school the colt, a skittish sort named *Babu's Baby*, in the saddling area.

After galloping once around the oval the following morning with Luke in the saddle, Skinner led the horse on the path from the gap of the racetrack toward the paddock. Prancing and walking sideways, the horse swung his head and swished his tail constantly. On his back, Luke talked to the fretting animal attempting to calm him down.

Once in the paddock, Skinner led *Babu's Baby* into one of the stalls and turned him around hoping the sweaty colt would settle down looking about and getting used to his new surroundings. Skinner gently cooed and patted the horse, when suddenly the animal reared up violently. In so doing, the lead line snatched from Skinner's hand. With his front legs flapping in the air, the horse lost his balance and flipped over backward, landing on Luke.

At age thirty-five, after riding thousands of horseraces, and considered by many one of the most talented East Coast jockeys of his generation, Luke suffered a fractured pelvis and a broken right leg, requiring multiple surgeries and a total reconstruction of his pelvis. As Caroline and his mother watched over him in the hospital, the premise of a little farm in Ocala was no longer on anyone's mind.

THE END

EPILOGUE

In his book *THE SPORT OF KINGS AND THE KINGS OF CRIME*, Steven A. Riess*, wrote: *"Thoroughbred racing was the first major sport in early America"* . . . *"Following the Civil War [thoroughbred racing], was one of the three great American spectator sports, along with baseball and boxing."*

However, long before that, thoroughbred racing was, and still is today, a microcosm of the larger world around it. Hundreds of thousands, even millions of lovers of the horse around the globe make the sport their lives' profession.

In today's great struggle for the entertainment dollar, the pageantry of racing continues to attract the masses. Purses have grown 100-fold, and international racing has become a reality with thoroughbreds from around the globe matching their speed on the world's biggest stages.

For all that, detractors of the industry perceive it as an unglamorous activity that generally sees horses enduring a miserable existence. When in reality, horses in a myriad of sporting events, and perhaps chief in thoroughbred racing, are among the most pampered and best cared for species in the animal kingdom.

Around the world, hundreds of organizations, many of those in the United States, see to the well-being of the horse and its people. They task to promulgate rules, promote integrity, and veterinary studies with the latest technology available. Stewards, the judges of racing, are perhaps more knowledgeable and experienced than ever before, with organizations entrusted to make this a fact, requiring continued education every two years to maintain current accreditation and experience.

And making sure that all the i's are dotted and every t is crossed, exists the up-to-the-minute focus of the most technically advanced media in history.

This being said, the preceding pages describe accounts that are the result of the author's vivid imagination. While the descriptions of the racetracks, towns and cities mentioned are as best memory serves, other places, events, personalities and names, are purely fictional and not intended to resemble anyone living or dead.

Finally, the astronomical amounts of money available to today's professional jockey, even one with limited talent, is an inducement to nullify the actions of the riders described herein. If integrity is the concept of consistency of actions, values, methods, measures, principles, expectations and outcomes, Luke Nodarse, and all like him, can be found in any jockeys' room in America.

*Steven A. Riess is the Bernard Brommel Distinguished Research Professor in the Department of History, Northeastern Illinois University, where he has taught over 35 years. He is the author of several books on the history of sports.

A former regular contributor to the racing section of the Miami News, and featured writer in other racing publications, Rene Riera, Jr. Born in Havana, Cuba, was one of the most popular jockeys in New England, during a riding career that began in 1968, under contract to trainer G. R. Handy, until 1971. From 1974-1977 was stable rider of the famed Spendthrift Farm. After retiring from riding in 1984, embarked in a career as a racing official, holding numerous important posts, including Racing Secretary and Director of Racing. Presently, he is a Racing Steward, and lives in Miami, Florida

www.ingramcontent.com/pod-product-compliance
Lightning Source LLC
Chambersburg PA
CBHW071702040426
42446CB00011B/1878